C000064296

'Packed with illustrati[...] will open up to you th[...] verse. Whether you wo[...], you will find yourself face to face with the beautiful God of love. It really could change your life.'
Jonty Allcock, Pastor, The Globe Church, London

'A banner with the words "John 3:16" continues to show up at many major sports events. Martin Salter gives a brilliant explanation of what it actually means. This short book is a very easy read, offering clarity about the Christian faith and loads of really simple and compelling illustrations that bring this famous Bible verse to life. I truly loved reading this book!'
Graham Daniels, General Director, Christians in Sport

'*So Loved* is a concise yet insightful exploration of some of the most famous words of Jesus. If you have questions about the Christian faith, you will find this book to be accessible, relatable and honest, and I encourage you to read it.'
Dr Sharon Dirckx, scientist, author and speaker

'In this warm and engaging little book, Martin Salter reveals the heart of the Christian message by walking through one of the best-loved verses in the Bible. If you are a sceptic or seeker, you will find food for thought. Martin answers questions, discusses big issues and tackles misconceptions with sensitivity, humour and clarity. He combines personal stories and references to contemporary culture and thinking, with helpful quotations from great

writers from the past, to provide a compelling case for the twenty-six words of John 3:16 being the best news for all people for all time.'
Clare Heath-Whyte, historian and author

'If you want a short and clear explanation of the good news that is the heart of Christianity, then this is the book for you. Contemporary illustrations spur your interest as Martin takes you through the best-known sentence in the Bible. I was impressed by the personal warmth speaking from the pages and the careful theology lying under the surface. John chapter 3, verse 16 tells the greatest story in the world, and Martin has done a wonderful job in showing just how vital this is for you and me.'
Andrew Hill, Executive Director, Soldiers' and Airmen's Scripture Readers Association

'A fresh, punchy, fascinating-facts-filled, humorous, yet thought-provoking take on the meaning of life, based on the Bible's most famous verse. Read it yourself and then pass it on to a friend. Go on. What do you have to lose?

'You'll also discover how woodpeckers avoid concussion (but I won't tell you which page that's on!).'
Jeremy McQuoid, Teaching Pastor, Deeside Christian Fellowship, Aberdeen, and Chairman of Trustees, Keswick Ministries

'Have you ever wanted to give something to a friend who's willing to be open-minded about the Christian faith and explore a bit further? Martin's book is friendly,

easy to read, personal and engaging. It walks us through perhaps the most famous verse in the Bible and, in doing so, summarizes the gospel comprehensively and accessibly.'
Jeremy Marshall, author and speaker

'Having been active in evangelism for more than twenty-five years, I share one verse more than any other: John 3:16. Timeless, relevant, widely familiar and simple to learn, it's a verse even a child can understand, and yet it's so deep that you cannot tire of studying it.

'Martin's book is a work of art: a mixture of theology, personal stories and lessons from history. It helps us not only to unpack but also to enjoy the richness of John 3:16. *So Loved* is for everyone: a wonderful one-to-one study to work through with a non-Christian friend, a reference for preachers, and a toolbox for fellow evangelists and apologists. It is a devotional, a commentary and a beautiful gift. If you are serious about evangelism, then you need to buy this book, a highlighter and a notepad – or the digital equivalent.'
Mitch, evangelist, Crown Jesus Ministries, Belfast

'As I read this, I thought of people I wanted to give it to. It's not a coincidence that this book is in your hand, and I really hope that you will read it. It is very relevant and – even more – important.'
George Verwer, Founder of Operation Mobilisation, author, missionary and speaker

Contents

Acknowledgments

I want to take this opportunity to express my gratitude for all the support and encouragement of family and friends throughout this process. I'm also grateful to all who read early versions of this book and offered helpful thoughts, comments and suggestions.

I'm thankful to my church family, who gave me a sabbatical during which the first draft of *So Loved* was written. I'm hugely grateful to Eleanor Trotter of IVP, who gave me so much time and attention to help me turn a rough-and-ready manuscript into the book you now hold in your hands.

Ultimately, I'm deeply and forever thankful to the God who so loved me that he gave his Son, that I might have eternal life.

Introduction: connecting to your deepest dreams

Elizabeth was ready to end it all. Abused as a child by a family member, unable to relate to her peers, angry, aggressive and self-harming, she left the house one evening with the sole intention of stepping out in front of a fast-moving lorry. As she stood on the pavement, a song from her childhood entered her mind: 'A sunbeam, a sunbeam, Jesus wants me for a sunbeam.'

It was ridiculous. Why would anyone want her – miserable and dirty – for a sunbeam? Yet she couldn't shake off this idea that there was a God who loved her and had a good plan for her life.

Forty years later, Elizabeth is still alive. She would be the first to tell you that there are still problems to overcome and hurts unhealed. But life has also been full of God's love, hope and light. A church leader once asked her to explain what had attracted her to God. 'That's easy,' she said. 'It was his love.'

It's amazing to think that there could be a God who knows us, loves us and has a plan for our lives. If you're someone who'd call yourself a sceptic, just pause for a moment. Consider what it would mean if that claim were true. This must be something worth exploring further, right?

The most famous verse in the Bible says:

For God so loved the world that he gave his one and only Son, that whoever believes in him shall not perish but have eternal life.
(John 3:16)

Stop. Read those words again. Pause. Read them one more time. Don't let any familiarity you might have with this verse dull the astonishing claim.

It truly is an astounding, mind-blowing, world-changing, life-transforming claim – and one that I didn't really understand for a long time.

As a kid, I was taken to church, but I turned my back on my parents' faith in my teens. Services were dull, boring and, as far as I could see, irrelevant. I lived my life by my own rules throughout my teenage years. It was only when I went to university that things changed. There, I found myself living in halls of residence and sharing a kitchen with two young Christian women. I can't pretend that my motives for spending time with them were entirely pure but, over time, I became intrigued. They really believed this faith stuff; it made a difference in their lives. And yet they were intelligent and thoughtful people.

I started to ask questions; then I started going along to church. As I investigated the Bible's message, I became increasingly convinced that this wasn't a book of made-up fairy tales but one that contained true stories of historical events. The Bible stood up to scrutiny – that was a revelation. There was evidence to back up its claims. It even made sense of my whole life and my world.

And so, during my first year at university, I became a Christian. I committed myself to believing and following the message of the Bible. As I look back now, I don't regret that decision for a second. I believe that Christianity is true, that it works and that it's the best decision I ever made. I now work for a church and spend much of my time thinking about how I can bring this wonderful message of life-changing love to others.

Come and look with me at the most famous verse in the Bible. It can be seen all over the world, in many different languages, on car stickers, fridge magnets, calendars, at football games and on the clothing, or even the faces, of international sporting stars.

But why is it so significant, important and cherished? What is it about those twenty-six words that has crossed continents and centuries, changing millions, if not billions, of lives? Why does this verse matter to us, to our world and to me in particular? Why am I so passionate about it?

It is because this verse speaks to our deepest hopes and dreams. It speaks to our desire for meaning, relationship, purpose and destiny. At the same time, it speaks against so much of the hate, despair, fear, greed and selfishness in our world.

It tells my heart that there is more to this life than simply what I can see, hear, touch, taste or smell. It tells me that I'm more than my salary or achievements, more than my job title or relationship status, more than my struggles and failures, and so much more than the verdict of my boss, friends, family or society. It tells me that I am known, valued and loved by someone much greater than I can fully comprehend. It tells me that all these things are not wishful thinking but true and real.

John 3:16 contains truth that centres everything else in my life.

We're going to take these famous words and consider them a section at a time. What do they mean? And why do they add up to the most important claim made by any person, at any time, in the whole of history?

1
For God . . .

For God so loved the world that he gave his one and only Son, that whoever believes in him shall not perish but have eternal life.'
(John 3:16)

Funerals can be devoid of hope.

I recently attended the funeral of a relative who'd requested a humanist service. This meant no reference to God, religion or an afterlife. We remembered his life, thanked him for it (as if he cared!), listened to his favourite piece of music, said our goodbyes and that was that. Everyone went to the pub for a sad-looking buffet – foil trays laid out with white triangular sandwiches containing some sweaty cheese, sprinkled with iceberg lettuce. There was no hope, no next life, no future reunions and no 'better place'. Nothing. Just an abrupt ending. A full stop to life. I felt cold and depressed. And the buffet made me sadder still.

John Lennon encouraged us to imagine a world without heaven or religion. He thought it would be a world of harmony and peace. But would it? Really?

Think for a moment about a world in which there was no God: a world with nothing more than what we see around us – no grand design and no ultimate purpose or meaning. We would be no more than the interaction of chemicals and the firing of neurons. There would be no point to anything. We would simply exist. Our sense of soul or spirit would be an illusion. And there would be no afterlife.

That doesn't sound so great to me.

But, then, simply wishing for a higher power doesn't make it true.

The opening words of John 3:16 begin with the most important claim for any human being to consider: namely, that there is a God.

Some of you won't need the rational explanations for the existence of a God. It is something you already believe and maybe always have done. You might not attend church or belong to a religious group but you would consider yourself spiritual. You resonate with the sense that 'there must be more than this'. Deep down you believe that there is a God but, perhaps, you're just not quite sure what such a God is like. Assuming you do need a little more convincing, though, let's consider two of the arguments for the existence of God.

1 Look around you

Did you know that

- a woodpecker can wrap its tongue around its brain to prevent it from becoming concussed when pecking a tree twenty times a second?

- a camel can drink up to a thousand pints of water in one go?
- a sperm whale can hold its breath for up to ninety minutes?

If you really want to blow your mind, think small:

- Your DNA, the building blocks of human life, if stretched out, could reach to the sun and back six hundred times.
- Almost two metres of DNA are squeezed into every cell.
- The coding of your DNA contains three billion letters – it would take fifty years to type it all out, filling a million pages.

In the light of this, it doesn't seem to be exaggerating to say that each and every life is a miracle.

Have you ever had a 'wow' moment? One that just takes your breath away?

I remember walking in the Lake District with a group of teenagers. After trudging uphill for hours, we were tired, hungry and wet. Finally, we reached the top, the weather cleared and – wow! – we were blown away by the view. No photograph could have fully captured the amazing sight of the countryside stretching out in every direction and our feeling of elation.

We live in a universe that astounds us with its beauty. We have all encountered moments of awe or wonder. At such times, we'll have experienced something more than just delight at creation. We'll have tasted a deeper sense of joy at life. We'll have felt somehow more alive.

We discover this 'wow' when watching sunsets and stargazing, when enjoying mountains and magnolias, when travelling in deserts or tasting desserts. The breadth and variety of life is absolutely astonishing. Whether we travel the globe or watch nature programmes from the comfort of our homes, our thirst for wonder is quenched by the 'wow' of our world.

And all of this is just on our little planet. We can't begin to get our heads around the scale of our universe. If we got on a plane tomorrow and took off for the sun, the journey would take us nineteen years. Yet our sun is just one star in a hundred million in our galaxy. Our galaxy is just one of a hundred million in our universe.

Where has all this 'wow' come from? Who or what caused our universe to exist?

If we're moderately familiar with science, I guess we might think the answer would be something such as the Big Bang and evolution.

Not so fast. The Big Bang and evolution are answers to a different question: the 'how' question. More specifically, they give explanations about *how* all the stuff was arranged as we currently see it.

I'm asking a different question. *Where* did the stuff or the energy come from in the first place?

If I were to bake a cake, scientists could explain the chemical reactions that turned yellow goo into tasty cake, but they couldn't say where I'd got the ingredients from. Also, they couldn't tell you *why* I made the cake.

The scientist Brian Cox was asked in an interview if he was an atheist. He replied that he didn't follow a particular religion but he couldn't call himself an atheist. Here's what he said:

> Science does not rule out the existence of a creator . . . We don't know how the universe began, full stop. That's it. We don't know. We have a theory of what might have happened before the Big Bang – a theory called inflation . . . but we're still left with the question, 'How did that start?' . . . Did the universe have a beginning and, if so, how did it begin? The answer is we don't know. Full stop. . . . From the scientific perspective, it is wrong to say that science has anything to say at all about the nature of a creator . . . because we don't know.[1]

So, scientists can't tell you *where* the universe came from, *why* it exists, or *who* or *what* the first cause was.

When my grandfather passed away, my mother came across an old pocket watch that had belonged to his father. It was a beautiful piece of craftsmanship. I took off the back and I could see the tiny cogs that made up the movement. It still works today, a hundred years after it was made. Nobody looking at it would think that it had made itself out of nothing. In the same way, the beauty and intricacy of our universe must point to the hand of a master craftsman.[2]

Anthony Flew was an atheist and a philosopher who, in later life, came to believe in the existence of a God.

9

One of the turning points for him was the existence of certain laws of nature that appeared to be exquisitely fine-tuned for life on earth.[3]

One example is something called the 'gravitational constant': the unchanging gravitational force that stops us all from floating away. If this force differed by 1 in 10^{60}, then life would be impossible. Scientists think there might be as many as twenty-six of these 'constants', each one finely tuned. If any were different, life on earth would be unsustainable.

If I played the lottery, the odds of my winning the jackpot would be enormously unlikely. If I won, you'd consider me extraordinarily lucky. If I then won the jackpot the next week and the week after that, you'd think I'd been cheating. But what if I won the jackpot twenty-six weeks running? How would you explain that?

The chances of our universe providing a home for humans are ridiculously small. The probability is similar to a huge number of blind people – enough to fill every football stadium in the world – all managing to solve their Rubik's cubes at exactly the same moment. It's like the chances of a tornado blowing through a scrapyard and assembling a Boeing 747.[4]

The physicist Albert Einstein wrote:

> We are in the position of a little child entering a huge library filled with books in many languages . . . the child dimly suspects a mysterious order in the arrangement of the books but doesn't

know what it is. That, it seems to me, is the attitude of even the most intelligent human being toward God. We see the universe marvellously arranged and obeying certain laws, but only dimly understand these laws.[5]

The evidence that God exists is all around us, from the stars to the subatomic. The universe's existence and design suggest that we're not here by accident.

2 Look inside yourself

This morning, as I was about to board a train, the lady in front of me dropped her phone from her bag without noticing. Not thinking, I picked it up and pocketed it.

I'm obviously joking. I gave it back. Of course. It never crossed my mind to pinch her phone. Is that because I'm a morally superior person or simply because humans have some kind of inbuilt moral compass? I suppose some people might have taken her phone, but most of us would condemn such an action. We instinctively know right from wrong.

So, where does this basic sense come from?

Human standards of right and wrong can be found in many different cultures. C. S. Lewis observed:

If anyone will take the trouble to compare the moral teaching of, say, the ancient Egyptians, Babylonians, Hindus, Chinese, Greeks and Romans, what will really strike him will be how very like they are to each other and to our own . . . For our present purpose I need only ask the reader to think what a totally different morality would mean. Think of a country where people were admired for running away in battle, or where a man felt proud of double-crossing all the people who had been kindest to him. You might just as well try to imagine a country where two and two made five.[6]

Where does that moral sense come from? And where do we get this thing called conscience – that inward sense of guilt or pride related to our own actions? Is it just the opinion of others that restrains us or is there something more within us?

Imagine life without God-given moral standards. Right and wrong would be the invention of groups of people for self-preservation. We could say that certain cultures had, at one time, deemed something wrong, but it wouldn't carry weight in other times. So something such as genocide could never by any *ultimate* standard be considered wrong. It would just be relatively un-acceptable to a particular society.

In 1887, Friedrich Nietzsche wrote *On the Genealogy of Morals* in which he objected to the idea of absolute moral standards. He believed that morals arise as the cry of the weak against the strong. He said, 'It is not surprising that the lambs should bear a grudge against the great birds of prey, but that is no reason for blaming the great birds of prey for taking the little lambs.'[7] He wasn't just talking about animals either.

For Nietzsche, the expressing of strength was a natural force and could only be considered otherwise by 'the errors of language'.[8] So the ideas of right and wrong are created by the weak in the interests of self-preservation. Nietzsche's ideas of the natural need for strength to exert itself became devastatingly influential among twentieth-century fascists, as historians will tell us.

Instinctively, we recognize his views to be misguided. We know there are things that are always and everywhere wrong.

It isn't just in the realm of morals that we can reach only a certain point in our explanations, but also in the realm of the beautiful. Remember 'Look around you' above? Where does our sense of wonder come from? And our enjoyment of all those things that move us deeply? So much seems to serve no evolutionary purpose. We may love live music or the theatre, and others enjoy art or poetry. It might be gardening, food or travel that inspire. All these possess a power to move us that cannot be explained by mere evolutionary biology. They seem to serve no valid purpose when it comes to the 'survival of the fittest'.

In *The Everlasting Man*, G. K. Chesterton considers the cave paintings attributed to early humans.[9] He challenges the view that prehistoric people were somehow savage and brutish. He looks at the paintings and asks where the impulse to create art came from. Is it right to consider a prehistoric individual a club-wielding, fire-making, bum-scratching, red-meat-eating thug? Is it not the case that the existence of primitive art demonstrates something deeper?

There is a particularly moving video of the conductor Benjamin Zander explaining his understanding of a piece of classical music by Frédéric Chopin.[10] He notes the progression of the music and its journey towards home. After explaining the piece, he plays it, leaving not a dry eye in the house. Put this book down and go and watch it . . .

Like me, you will have had those experiences in which something lovely or beautiful has brought a tear to your eye. Is it not possible that moments such as those are evidence of the handprint of God on your soul?

John 3:16 begins with a bold claim about the existence of a God. You might disagree. Yet the evidence *around* us and *within* us – the claims of nature, order, beauty and morality – make that claim seem believable. There is a God. I'm convinced of it.

So what kind of God is he? If there is a God, what is he like?

2

So loved . . .

> For God **so loved** the world that he gave his one
> and only Son, that whoever believes in him shall
> not perish but have eternal life.
> (John 3:16)

Have you ever played a word association game, when
someone says a word and you follow with the first thing
that comes into your head? For example, someone says
'fish' and you reply 'chips'; someone says 'beach' and you
say 'sandcastle'; or someone says 'England football team'
and you say 'disappointment'.

If we were to play now and I were to start with the
word 'God', what would you reply?

For some, God is distant and uncaring. If there is a
God, then he is so remote that he is not really involved
in this world at all. How else could we account for the
grief, suffering and pain all around us? Even if he were
interested, surely, he's got bigger things to worry about
than my little life?

For other people, God is a harsh headmaster or dom-
ineering parent – someone who can never be pleased,
and is constantly watching and waiting for ways to catch
us out and tell us off. This God is a disciplinarian task-
master, not a God of love.

For yet others, God is a kind, grandfatherly figure. He is favourably disposed towards us, but his capacity to *do* much about our struggles is limited. He watches on, longing for better things, but he's unable to change much at all.

And, again, for others, God is a mystery. We hope he's watching over us and will one day let us into heaven, but we don't really know. Maybe we don't mind not knowing; perhaps we think we simply cannot know.

I think the Gospel writer John would tell us that none of these views properly captures the nature of God. He tells us that God isn't distant, a harsh disciplinarian or a benign grandfather, and he isn't an unfathomable mystery.

Does that surprise you? John's next claim is that the God who lives is the God who *loves*: 'For God so *loved* the world.'

That prompts another question: what does it mean to say that God is a God of love?

Love means . . .

Someone asked a group of 7- to 9-year-olds about their understanding of the word 'love'. Here's their wisdom:

- 'Shake your hips and hope for the best' (Matt, aged 8).
- 'Tell your wife that she looks pretty, even if she looks like a truck!' (Ricky, aged 7).

- 'Love is like an avalanche, where you have to run for your life' (John, aged 9).
- 'Love is the most important thing in the world, but baseball is pretty good, too' (Greg, aged 8).[1]

We all have our own understanding of the word 'love', and it can also have a range of meanings depending on the way we use it. For example, I *love* prawn-cocktail crisps; I *love* my wife and kids; I *love* cricket, football and running (and most sports, to be honest); I *love* my brother; and I *love* the *Pitch Perfect* films (don't judge me). However, these loves aren't all the same. My love for my family is of a different sort from the love I have for crisps. If I had to choose between my wife and scampi fries, well, the answer is obvious, isn't it?

Not only are our loves different but they also vary in intensity and duration. Sometimes we love for a time or the object of our love changes. We talk about falling in and out of love. Love in our culture is often associated with feelings rather than decisions of the will.

Sometimes, love goes horribly wrong. We find that we don't love others as we should or others don't love us as we'd hoped. Despite Hollywood's romantic ideal, human love is often broken.

The Office for National Statistics (ONS) recorded more than ninety thousand divorces in England and Wales in 2018.[2] That's almost one every five minutes. Around 42% of marriages in England and Wales end in divorce.[3]

My own parents divorced when I was 19, so I know that these aren't just statistics. Each number represents heartbreak, grief and painful memories. Children are affected, with their own understanding of love being shaped in the process. If we've been hurt by others, it's easy to close ourselves off from the possibility of love.

It's not surprising that many people struggle with the idea of a loving God. What *sort* of love does God have for humans?

We might think that God's love is like our own – changeable and fleeting. Or we may think that God loves us in the same way a mother loves a wayward child: she loves him but she may not always like him very much. Maybe that's how you think about God's love.

I often struggle with this. I often fall into thinking God's love for me is based on how well I'm obeying him. When I stumble, I imagine him frowning like a disappointed PE teacher: 'Fluffed it again, Salter!' When we were at school, we all knew that PE teachers loved certain kids, but the rest of us would feel their disapproving gaze. Is God like that? Does he love the squeaky-clean religious types but despair of the rest of us? What does it actually *mean* to say God loves me?

A different type of love

In some ways, human love is a picture of God's love because we are made in his image. In other ways, though, God's love is not like ours. His love is perfect. It is eternal and unchanging. As one writer has rightly said, God's love is a 'truth that is simple enough for a small child to grasp and yet deep enough to occupy us for eternity'.[4]

To help us think about this further, we're going to consider a quote from an older writer called John Owen. He was a seventeenth-century church leader in England. He wrote many books and is known for his deep reflections. Admittedly, his language is a little harder for us moderns to read, but it's worth looking past that for some really important ideas.

He writes about our verse – John 3:16 – and describes God's love as having

> such an earnest, intense affection, consisting in an eternal, unchangeable act and purpose of his will, for the bestowing of the chiefest good.[5]

OK, so it's not the snappiest soundbite out there, but notice the different elements in John Owen's description.

God's love is *more*

My kids used to enjoy a book called *Guess How Much I Love You*.[6] Big Nutbrown Hare and Little Nutbrown Hare are describing their love for each other. Little Nutbrown Hare says, 'I love you as high as I can hop.' To which Big Nutbrown Hare replies, 'I love you as high as *I* can hop.' Little Nutbrown Hare stretches out his arms and says, 'I love you this much.' Big Nutbrown Hare stretches out his arms and says, 'I love you *this* much.' Little Nutbrown Hare thinks, 'Mmm, that is a lot.' The final pages show Little Nutbrown Hare attempting one last go at outdoing Big Nutbrown Hare. He says, 'I love you to the moon,' and then falls asleep in Big Nutbrown Hare's arms. Big Nutbrown Hare looks down at the sleeping Little Nutbrown Hare and says, 'I love you to the moon – and back.'

Look at the John Owen quote again. Notice that it begins by describing God's love has having an 'earnest, intense affection'.

As a Christian, I believe human beings are made in the image of God. Part of that is to reflect (imperfectly) some of his qualities. When we talk about human goodness, wisdom or love, we are describing something that finds its perfect expression in God. When we talk about God's love, we are talking about a love that is the most perfect and complete expression of love in existence.

As one writer puts it:

> Understood rightly, God has not less, but infinitely more, affection than any of his creatures . . . God is immeasurably more emotionally alive than any other being . . . It is because God loves so much that his love is not like a human passion.[7]

Isn't that amazing? Stop and let it sink in . . .

Whatever our human conception of love, it pales by comparison with God's love. We can scarcely begin to imagine or describe the immensity of what it means to say that God is a God of love. What is truly breathtaking is that all of that love is directed towards people like you and me.

God's love is for ever

Owen describes God's love as an 'eternal, unchangeable act and purpose of his will'. God exists outside space and time. He isn't thrown by changing seasons and circumstances. There is no new information that alters his feelings about us.

Part of our difficulty here is that we tend to think of God as being like a really big, strong superhuman – like you and me but just scaled up. Like the best Marvel Avenger, with awesome superpowers. However, the Bible gives us a much more mind-blowing picture: a God who is uncreated, outside time and space, all-knowing, all-powerful, ever-present, good, loving, holy and just. God is love in his very being. Within the eternal Trinity – the three persons of God: Father, Son and Holy Spirit – perfect love has always existed.

John says, 'God is love' (1 John 4:8). Do you notice that it's not just that love is a feeling God has – it's who he is? It's part of his essence and character. God's love is his eternal settled decision and his total commitment towards us. It's the unfailing spring of his being flowing out towards us. It cannot be extinguished, redirected or altered. It is who he chooses to be towards the creation he has made.

God's love never changes

A team of scientists from the National Institute for Standards and Technology in Boulder, Colorado, built a new sort of atomic clock, which they termed an 'optical

clock'. I don't pretend to understand the science involved, but the claim is that it is so accurate it won't gain
or lose more than a single second every fourteen billion
years. Sadly, none of us will be around to find out if
it's true!

Contrast that with an old grandfather clock. The
most accurate of these was reckoned to gain or lose
around a minute a week. That's still pretty impressive,
but you can see how little time it might take for these
clocks to become significantly inaccurate. A minute a
week would be almost five in a month, and as much as
an hour in a year. In just one year, if not corrected, your
clock could be significantly off. If you were relying on
this clock for your New Year's Eve countdown, you
might well miss it.

John Owen describes God's love as the '*unchangeable*
act and purpose of his will'. God's love isn't a fleeting
emotion that may come and go. The Bible ties the intense
and earnest affection together with God's purpose and
will. So often our human love is subject to change in
terms of its intensity and its object. It's a feeling that can
come and go. If we fall out of love with someone, then
we end a relationship. God's love is different: it is as
much about the decision of his will as it is his earnest
and intense affection.

Human love can often be the grandfather clock –
changeable and unreliable. Divine love is like the atomic
clock – always steady, always sure, always reliable. Love
is not a fleeting affection, but 'a steady wish for the loved
person's ultimate good'.[8]

22

God's love seeks us out

Finally, Owen describes the aim of God's love: 'the bestowing [giving] of the chiefest good'.

We're getting slightly ahead of ourselves here. We'll think more about the object of God's love in the next chapter. However, it is worth pausing briefly at this point to notice the aim of God's love – 'the bestowing of the chiefest good'.

Jesus told a story about a prodigal son who ran away from home, blew it big time, and had no choice but to come home and face the consequences. Jesus tells us, 'While he was still a long way off, his father saw him and was filled with compassion for him; he ran to his son, threw his arms round him and kissed him' (Luke 15:20). He doesn't stand far off, aloof, waiting for the son to grovel. No. The father is on the run while the son still can't lift his head. The story is not so much about the prodigal son as it is about the love of the father.

A little more than two decades ago, I trained as a nurse and did a number of hospital placements. Occasionally, on a set of patient notes would be the letters 'DNR' for 'Do Not Resuscitate'. Sometimes, a patient would be so poorly that to attempt resuscitation in the event of a cardiac arrest would cause greater harm and distress. Such cases were obviously difficult for patients and their families to come to terms with. DNR was also difficult for medical staff. However, sometimes, for good reasons, this was the best course of action.

But God has no stack of DNR files. There are no cases beyond the love of God.

Perhaps the real human problem with divine love is that we're reluctant to open ourselves up to such love. Previous experience may have made us suspicious, hard or closed. But God's love bids you welcome and draws near even as you seek retreat.

John Owen's description of God's love is truly wonderful, if we stop to think about it. Let it sink in: God's love is his

> earnest, intense affection, consisting in an eternal, unchangeable act and purpose of his will, for the bestowing of the chiefest good.[9]

OK, it's old-fashioned language. You have to translate it in your head. Maybe you think it a bit quaint. But it aims to describe the barely describable – the immense, immeasurable, infinite love that is nothing less than God himself. Elsewhere, John Owen said that the greatest unkindness we can do to God is not believe that he loves us.

God is not distant, uncaring or harsh. He is the perfection of all that we call love. And the object of his love? Read on!

3

The world . . .

> For God so loved **the world** that he gave his one
> and only Son, that whoever believes in him shall
> not perish but have eternal life.
> (John 3:16)

I enjoy food – all kinds. I love discovering new foods
and flavours, and will eat and enjoy almost anything
(although I do consider mushrooms an abomination).
My kids, on the other hand, can be fussier. If you were
to ask them whether they love food, they'd reply, '*Some*
food.' There are a few things they love, some they tolerate
and others they'll complain about.

Is God's love for people like my children's love of
food? Does God love some people, tolerate others and
dislike the rest?

If I were to ask you *whom* God loves, how might you
reply?

I suspect many people would intuitively think God
loves religious people, good people and kind people.
Captain Sir Tom Moore raised more than £30 million
for the National Health Service by walking laps of his
garden ahead of his one hundredth birthday. God *loves*
people like that, right?

But what if we flipped the question and asked whether
there are people whom God does *not* love? On 22 July

2011, Anders Breivik put on a police uniform, took a ferry to the Norwegian island of Utøya and opened fire, killing sixty-nine people, most of whom were students. God couldn't *love* someone like that, could he?

John claims that God loves the *world*. That's quite a claim. We'll have to think some more about what that actually means. But notice that the verse doesn't say, 'For God so loved Christians', or, 'For God so loved the sincere'. It says 'the world'.

God's love for people is not like my kids' selective love of food. God doesn't like some types of people, tolerate others and dislike the rest. God loves *all* kinds of people. This idea would have been a shock to people in the ancient world, hearing it for the first time. Many in Jesus' day would have thought that the devout and the religious leaders were especially loved by God: the priests, the leaders and the teachers. Surely these were the people God *really* loved? The tax collectors, beggars and prostitutes? Not so much.

Jesus told a story of two men who went to the temple to pray.[1] The first, a religious leader, looked up to heaven and thanked God that he was such a decent, upstanding chap – not like the 'robbers, evildoers [and] adulterers' (Luke 18:11). He was the sort of guy who fasts twice a week and gives a tenth of his money to the poor. The second, a tax collector, stood at a distance and looked at the floor. He beat his chest and said, 'God, have mercy on me, a sinner' (Luke 18:13). People in Jesus' day thought God's love was only really for good, upstanding religious types, like the first man.

So the words of John 3:16 would have been shocking, perhaps even disturbing – God loves *the world*? Really? Even the surrounding nations? What about those awful Romans occupying the land and suppressing their freedoms? Even them? Yes, even them. God's love knows no borders or barriers. It extends across territories and tribes. God's love is directed at the *world* – rich, poor, male, female, slave, free, black, white, good people and, yes, even bad people. And on, to individuals like you and me.

This is a huge claim. We need to dig a little deeper to understand fully what is meant here by 'world'.

Defining 'English' and 'worldish'

In 2004, Kate Fox wrote *Watching the English: The hidden rules of English behaviour*. She observed several characteristics that she suggested define Englishness: a love of self-deprecating humour, a dislike of fuss, chronic pessimism, an unwillingness to talk about money, the importance of fair play, and the values of courtesy and modesty.[2]

As an Englishman, I've met a number of Americans who say how much they love the 'English'. Maybe they're just being polite, but what exactly do they mean? I don't think they're talking about love for each and every individual who lives or was born in the place we call England. I think it's really a statement about *English-ness*. They mean a love for certain English values and culture – the sorts of things Kate Fox describes. We might add to the list a cup of tea, the Queen, the accent, the 'stiff upper lip' and the love of an orderly queue. The statement 'I love the English' would refer more to the collective culture than to each and every English citizen.

We need to consider how John uses the word 'world' to help us to understand what he means here in saying that 'God so loved the world'.

In John's account of Jesus' life, Jesus says several striking things about the 'world'.

Jesus says that the 'world' hates him (John 7:7).

This clearly cannot refer to every human individual, as many did accept Jesus' message and follow him.

Jesus says that the 'world' will hate the disciples, too (John 17:14).

Again, this cannot refer to every human being. Many people believed the message and joined the followers.

Jesus says that the disciples do not belong to the 'world', just as Jesus does not belong to the 'world' (John 17:16).

In a sense, of course, the disciples are of the world, but not in the way that Jesus intends.

So it seems that something deeper is going on with the term 'world' – it can't refer to each and every person.

It seems to be used, like our earlier example of the 'English', to refer to something like a collective culture of beliefs, attitudes and values.

Here's what I think John means: *the 'world' stands for people who have rejected God and his Son, Jesus.* That makes sense of the quotes above from Jesus, doesn't it?

As John uses the term 'world', it seems often to have a spiritual meaning. It isn't so much about geography or population. In John's usage, 'world' refers to humanity in rebellion against God.

In some ways, it makes the claim that God loves the world even more extraordinary. Unlike my American friends' love for English culture, God's love is extended towards something basically negative – a 'world' that has set itself against him.

Remarkably, God sees people who have pushed him away and want little to do with him, and yet he still loves them with an earnest and intense affection. Isn't that an amazing thought?

Admittedly, some of this sounds strange to our ears as modern readers. You may think that such a description of the 'world' does not fit you very well. Let's consider the primary problem of the 'worldish'. It's summed up in another word often riddled with mis-understanding: *sin*.

Defining sin

When I was a kid, I once tried running away. I packed a little bag, walked out through the door, wandered down the street and across the road, and sat in the park. After about ten minutes, I decided I'd had enough and that I'd made my point. Actually, I started to get scared and so I went back home. I'm not sure that my mum had noticed I'd gone.

I don't even remember why I decided to try to run away. I suspect I'd received a telling-off and got the hump. You don't need to have children to know there is something within all of us that dislikes being told what to do. We want to be the masters of our fate and the captains of our souls.[3]

John uses 'world' to depict human beings rejecting God and rebelling against him. The Bible uses another word for such rejection and rebellion: 'sin'.

I like Francis Spufford's colourful way of defining sin, which I'll paraphrase as *the human propensity to mess things up.*[4] Human beings, as individuals and collectively, seem to have a peculiar talent for breaking stuff – in ourselves, in others, in relationships and in our world. The human potential for genius is matched only by our potential for evil.

However, as much as I like Spufford's way of putting things, his definition doesn't quite capture the root of 'sin'. He never gets to the origin of our rebellious streak. Exactly *why* are we so good at messing things up?

I suggest we tend to be good at this because we distance ourselves from God's rule and his care. Our desire to be independent means that we wander away from what is best for us. We all suffer from 'Sinatra syndrome' – each of us living life 'my way'. It's like taking the instructions for flatpack furniture and tossing them into a bin, saying, 'Don't patronize me. I know how to build stuff.' It never usually ends well.

It is because we reject God and follow our own paths that we end up in places where we hurt ourselves and others, and in the process offend a holy God who wants the best for us.

The 'sin' that characterizes the 'world' is a wrong attitude towards God. We can be like grumpy teenagers telling our parents to get lost, although, let's be honest, we clothe our rejection of God in more sophisticated dress.

A long time ago, a Christian leader called Augustine memorably described the rebellious nature of the human heart. He described an occasion when, as a child, he stole some pears (they'd run out of pick 'n' mix at his local shop). He reflected:

> Those pears were truly pleasant to the sight, but it was not for them that my miserable soul lusted, for I had an abundance of better pears. I stole them simply that I might steal, for having stolen them, I threw them away. My sole gratification in them was my own sin, which I was pleased to enjoy.[5]

Augustine suggests that what was going on here was his own heart's desire for rebellion, for freedom, for life outside other people's rules.

The Bible word 'sin' is about far more than simply rule-breaking. It describes a deep attitude of the heart.

31

Now, we know that our personal independence and freedom are good things. They enable us to live our lives without being forced by others to act against our will. However, sometimes what we call independence is really another word for a sort of proud self-determination. We put ourselves above the criticism or correction of others. We find it easy to spot the speck in someone else's eye, but we're not always quite so quick to see the plank in our own.[6]

If we're honest, we have to confess that there are times when we are carried away with our own sense of self-importance. It's why we always look for our own faces in the group photo. It's why we love it when the topic of conversation is ourselves. It's why the first thing we do with social media is to check the notifications regarding our own status updates.

Humans have achieved amazing things in the sciences and in the arts. But we've also done horrific things. What is true of the whole is also true of the individual. While it is painful, it is sometimes necessary to take an honest look at how we stand, particularly in relation to the God who made us.

Sin is a sort of vandalism – a defacing of the good. We take God's good gifts and often use them towards less-than-good ends. Here's how one writer describes it:

The intelligence of Nazi commanders came from God. The truth portion of an effective lie makes the lie plausible. The physical power of the assail-ant comes from the gift of good health. In the

Harry Potter series, the Dark Lord, He-Who-Must-Not-Be-Named, could not be an evil genius without being a genius.[7]

In this sense, our sin is parasitic on the good. The poet John Donne wrote, 'O Lord, thou hast set up many candlesticks, and kindled many lamps in me, but I have either blown them out, or carried them to guide me in forbidden ways.'[8] We use God's light to lead ourselves into dark places.

Corruption turns God's gifts away from their intended purposes. And this vandalism of the good doesn't happen in isolation. Our lives interact with other lives in communities, and cultures are formed as a result:

Sinful lives intersect with sinful lives . . . where the waves meet, cultures form. In a racist culture, racism will look normal. In a secular culture, indifference toward God will look normal . . . whole matrices of evil appear in which various forms of wrongdoing cross-pollinate and breed.[9]

The Bible uses many pictures to describe sin. We have seen it as rebellion, as independence, as pride and as vandalism. These are replicated, multiplied, by individuals, across generations and cultures. This is sin. And this is the main problem bound up in the 'world'.

It's this sin, pride, rebelliousness and brokenness that is present in my heart and makes me part of that 'world'.

Amazingly, it's this sin, pride, rebelliousness and broken-ness that God responds towards in love.

For God so loved **the world** . . .

Flick back to John Owen in the previous chapter. Love seeks our highest good.

The question then must be: what does God *do* out of his love for this rebellious world?

4

That he gave . . .

> For God so loved the world **that he gave** his one
> and only Son, that whoever believes in him shall
> not perish but have eternal life.
> (John 3:16)

It was Christmas morning, and I was 10 years old. I'd
been awake since 5 a.m. I couldn't wait for my parents
to wake up so that I could open my presents. There was
one present that I was really hoping to receive. I'd been
nagging for a while, and, in the weeks before Christmas,
I'd caught glimpses of strange and bulky shapes in my
parents' wardrobe that had fuelled my excitement.

It wasn't an especially expensive gift, although I
suspect my parents had to stretch the budget to buy it.
As I raced down the stairs, I couldn't contain my
excitement as I spied its unmistakable form, wrapped,
in the corner of the room. This began a journey for me.
That gift is still with me today, standing in the corner of
our bedroom – much to my wife's delight! It was my first
guitar.

It's not the most expensive guitar in the world – far
from it – but its value to me is not in its monetary worth,
but in the fact that my parents knew what I wanted and
went out of their way to buy it. There are much more

expensive guitars in the world but this one is special to me because of who gave it – the kind of gift I don't think I'll ever get rid of.

Everyone loves a thoughtful and well-chosen gift. There's something special about someone who knows us, taking the time to consider what we're like and what we like, and finding something of worth and value to us.

The idea of 'gift' is one of the most important in the Christian faith. In the Bible, it's often called 'grace'. It's the idea that God *gives* us the greatest gift, even though we've done nothing at all to earn or deserve such a gift. It is a gift freely given out of God's love for us.

But gifts aren't always straightforward, are they?

Is it a gift or are there strings attached?

In our culture, gifts often come with invisible strings attached. Some of us may have had the experience of someone we know using gifts to manipulate or control. Gifts are sometimes used in business to secure or sweeten a deal. And then there's the awkward issue of how much to spend on a friend's birthday present, which might be determined in part by how much they have spent on ours. Gift giving can end up as a complex social game, with unspoken rules, that has the power to make or break relationships. As a result, we can be suspicious of any talk of a *completely* free gift with no strings attached.

The situation was even more complex in the ancient world in which John wrote his Gospel. In the cultures of Ancient Greece and Rome, gift giving *always* came with strings attached. The ancient writer Seneca wrote a bestselling page-turner about the social rules around the giving and receiving of gifts. People maintained or improved their social status with a complex set of reciprocal relationships. A wealthy or influential Roman citizen might provide legal help and protection to certain members of the lower classes. In return, the latter would provide support for his political campaign.[1] This was called a patron–client relationship. The more clients a patron had, the more important he was considered to be. The clients would provide the patron with an entourage as he wandered around the city every morning, thereby demonstrating his social importance. In return, the client might be rewarded with some food for his family[2] or could even be invited to dinner with the patron, but only to make up the numbers. The clients would be seated in the less honourable seats and given cheap wine. Sometimes they were there to be the butt of jokes. This sort of 'friendship' and gift giving doesn't seem particularly generous or kind-hearted.

It is easy to see that this sort of relationship wasn't really one of gift and friendship but, rather, one of worker and wages. This was common across the Roman Empire. Many resented the idea of giving gifts at all. One wrote, 'I hate poor people. If anyone wants something for nothing, he's a fool. Let him pay up and he'll get it.'[3]

So this was the mindset of the ancient world, where the idea of getting something for nothing was alien. The idea of God's gift or grace was a radical, even offensive, concept in a culture of reciprocity. The idea that something could be given with no strings attached, requiring nothing in return, just as a gift – a pure gift – would have sounded incredible, even foolish, to an ancient ear.

This mindset also features in many people's concept of religion. The idea of the freely given gift is contrary to how many people think of a relationship with God.

Is it a gift if it's earned?

Many today think that God's gift is something that we must earn through effort, devotion or good works. If we do enough good deeds and don't break too many rules, then we'll put enough credit in our 'God-account' to receive his gift of heaven when we die. When God weighs our good against our bad, we hope the scale will tip the right way. Of course, that would not really be a gift at all. It would be something we had earned ourselves.

Many *religions* work in just this way. The world religions with which we are familiar today can be split into two major families:

1 the monotheistic Abrahamic religions (Judaism, Christianity and Islam);
2 the Eastern polytheistic (that is, with many gods) and Indian religions (such as Hinduism, Buddhism and Sikhism).

All of these have in common some kind of ultimate goal, which, however, is understood in different ways. Sometimes, the aim is enlightenment or 'nirvana'. Sometimes, it's heaven or paradise.

The Abrahamic faiths (1) have largely considered true worship and devoted obedience to be what deserves rewards. In Judaism, the proper observance of the Jewish law merits God's favour. In Islam, paradise is achieved through following the Five Pillars[4] and worshipping Allah alone. In some forms of Christianity, people believe that heaven is achieved if they perform certain rituals or if they spend time in a post-mortem place where they cleanse themselves of their sins (commonly known as purgatory).[5] (*Spoiler alert*: I am going to disagree strongly with this portrayal of what it means for a Christian to find eternal life.)

The Eastern religions (2) have tended to define religion as a journey towards enlightenment, achieved through devotion, meditation and deeds of service. In Hinduism, for example, salvation is achieved through the way of works, the way of knowledge or the way of devotion. The soul passes through cycles of lives, with the next incarnation dependent on the previous one. The ultimate goal is *moksha*, which is the release from the cycles of rebirth, achieved when the soul has overcome all ignorance and desire. In Buddhism, nirvana comes through following the eightfold path[6] towards enlightenment. In essence, it's the effort and devotion of the worshipper that determines the path.

In all these, God isn't giving a gift; he's simply rewarding effort. In all but one of these religions, the ultimate goal is achieved, at least in part, by the religious performance of the worshipper.

It is only in the Bible's teaching that we find God *giving freely* the gift of salvation and eternal life: 'God so loved the world that he *gave*' . . . no earning, no merit, no reward according to effort – a free gift with no strings attached, available to anyone who will receive it. (It is worth saying, at this point, that this isn't quite the whole story. There *is* a huge cost involved *but* it isn't paid for by us. More later.)

Is it a gift if I deserve it?

My wife is wrong. I'm really an outstanding driver. Yes, it may have taken me five attempts to pass my driving test, but who's counting? Actually, I *was*. My mates all passed first or second time, and I was anxious not to be left behind. What was wrong with me? I absolutely dreaded the practical exam. The theory part was fine. But I hated being watched. The critical gaze of the examiner, watching for every mistake, made my palms sweat, my heart race and my stomach knot. I found the experience totally debilitating.

I've met people who think that a relationship with God is a bit like a relationship with a driving examiner. God is sitting in the metaphorical passenger seat, noting down all our minor and major faults. But if that were the case, there would only be one outcome, right?

Sadly, the view of religion that says God's favour can be earned leads to one of three undesirable outcomes:

1 You may think you've failed to make the grade, give up and feel like a worthless failure.
2 You may try as hard as you can, still come up short and feel resentment towards the God who seems impossible to please.
3 You may think that you've succeeded, that God is now somehow in your debt, and that he owes you for your effort, success and achievement.

None of these three seems to be a relationship of love and friendship. None seems to have at its heart a desire for human flourishing. All leave us somehow less fulfilled, less grateful and maybe even less human in the end.

Think about human relationships for a moment. Is love something you can ever really earn or buy? Do you truly want the love of your spouse to be dependent on the size of your salary? Do you want the love of a parent to be earned from your career success? I think most of us would recognize such relationships to be dysfunctional or even toxic.

If we think about it, how much of what we have is all down to us anyway? When we take exams, how much of our success (or lack of it) is our own? To some degree, success depends on the quality of the school, the pushiness of our parents, the encouragement of our teachers, the influence of our peers and the natural abilities that we've inherited.

The careers we pursue are all results of these early influences, our personalities and often our circumstances. The job I now have was, in part, dependent on a chance meeting. The opportunities that come our way are often linked to forces beyond our control. We like to think we deserve a certain wage and that we've earned the life we enjoy, but to what extent is our deserving based purely on ourselves? Can we really determine our own destiny?

I'm posing these questions merely to illustrate that a view of life or religion that situates success or failure purely and solely in me, as an individual, is a burden too great to bear.

I wonder if you've ever thought about the idea that we all have certain 'gods' we live for. If you stop to think about it, there are things in all our lives that occupy 'divine' space, that we think will meet our deep needs and hopes. It may be money. You might work hard to earn money in the belief that it will provide what you most want and need. It may be a relationship. You may pursue 'the one' in the belief that such a person will make you truly complete. You may chase success (whatever that looks like) in the hope that it will satisfy your deepest needs for affirmation and a sense of purpose.

If you chase any of these things, then they are your functional gods. You work for them in the hope that they will reward you. They *gift* you nothing. They *grace* you with nothing. But you serve them nonetheless, hoping that one day they'll reward your effort. These gods are the opposite of the God that John presents. You serve your gods in the hope of reward. The one true God gives but needs nothing in return. The grace of God has no bonus scheme or performance-related pay. It's neither a medal for prowess nor an honour recognizing your community contribution. It's free – no strings attached.

Gift and grace

When my wife Sarah and I were in our mid twenties, we went through a significant life change. We'd just had our first child, and we were about to finish working for a church and head off to theological college for three years. We were also having some car trouble. My Renault 19, although it boasted the luxury of a sun-roof, a working CD player and electric windows, was hopelessly unreliable. In fact, the breakdown company eventually refused to keep coming out as I'd phoned them too many times. At this point, some friends decided they would like to give us their old car, which they were replacing. When I say 'old car', it was much nicer and newer than any we had ever owned! We were blown away by their kindness and generosity. There were no strings attached – it was simply a free gift prompted by their care for us.

The truth that God 'gave' stands opposed to the idea that I earn, and it liberates us human beings from the slavery of self-sufficiency. In all other religions, our eternal happiness is something we achieve, not something we receive. But this isn't the way the Bible speaks about the relationship between us and God; there's no contract whereby we are obliged to do (or not do) certain things in return for reward. It is a relationship of love in which God gladly gives us what we could never earn or deserve. It is simply a gift.

If we flick back to chapter 2, we see that it is only because of God's eternal, unchanging love, which seeks our highest good, that he gives. And in chapter 3, we see that this love extends to the 'world': the human race running hard in rebellion against God's kind rule and care.

But there's another reason why earning just cannot work. We never could earn God's favour when we so often live our lives independently of him. He makes the first move, in love, towards us while we are still far off (remember the prodigal son?). He simply gives, even to a world that would naturally reject the gift.

It isn't that there are two ways to pursue God's favour through religion: to work for it or to receive it as a gift. There is only really one. The former can never deliver, so we are wholly dependent on the latter. If it were not for God's gracious gift to us, we could never earn eternal life in our own strength.

I'd love a Ferrari (I am, after all, an outstanding driver). But the truth is that I could never afford to insure, let alone buy, one. So either someone else pays for the car and the insurance and gives it to me as a gift or I'll never have one. It's as simple as that. Likewise, I cannot earn God's love and acceptance through effort. It is something he chooses freely to give me. It is either rejected or received but never achieved.

And God isn't a begrudging giver either. If we're honest, I guess many of us will have somebody within our circle to whom we give gifts out of a sense of duty. We think that we must. Maybe he gets us something, so we feel that we must return the favour. We then get caught in the trap of trying to work out how little we can give without appearing mean or tight-fisted (and I don't think that's just me).

God doesn't give because he feels under compulsion to do so; he gives out of the eternal disposition of love. Nor does he give to gain in return; he doesn't need anything from us. God sees our need and, moved by compassion, gives us what we most need (we'll read more about what that is in the following chapters).

This is grace. It is this grace that makes us grateful human beings. It makes us generous. It makes us humble. Grace transforms and changes everything in our lives as we recognize the undeserved kindness of an almighty and gracious God towards us.

John Newton was born in London in 1725. One biographer describes him as a 'wild and angry young man who rebelled against authority at every opportunity'.[7] When he was 18, he was press-ganged into the navy, where his rule-breaking earned him a public flogging. At one point, he contemplated murdering the captain and committing suicide by throwing himself overboard. He said of himself, 'I was exceedingly vile . . . I not only sinned with a high hand myself but made it my study to tempt and seduce others.'[8] Later, Newton worked on slave ships and then for a slave-trader. He mistreated others and suffered mistreatment himself. He became a hardened and aggressive atheist.

It was on board a slave ship that he picked up a Christian book and, out of boredom, began to read. He began to worry that its words might be true. That same night, the ship was caught in a terrible storm and Newton cried out to God. After this point, he began to think more about his life, to read the Bible and pray.[9] A while later, he left the slave ships and became a preacher, ordained in the Church of England, and a hymn writer, eventually joining William Wilberforce in the campaign to abolish the slave trade.

In December 1772, Newton prepared a New Year's Day message based on the words of a prayer of David, a king of Ancient Israel, which begins, 'Who am I, Sovereign LORD, and what is my family, that you have brought me this far?' (2 Samuel 7:18). He also wrote a hymn for the occasion, reinforcing the message of his sermon and echoing something of his own story.[10] The first verse says:

> Amazing grace! How sweet the sound
> that saved a wretch like me!
> I once was lost, but now am found;
> was blind, but now I see.

Newton had fully grasped what he wished others to understand: God, in his love for the world, *gave*.

Truly, this is amazing grace.

5

His one and only Son . . .

> For God so loved the world that he gave **his one and only Son**, that whoever believes in him shall not perish but have eternal life.
> (John 3:16)

In Greek mythology, King Minos of Crete was the most powerful and revered man in the world. During a war with Athens, he sent his son Androgeus with terms of peace. He thought the people of Athens would respect his son and that peace could be achieved. Sadly, however, Androgeus was not well received but rather murdered, triggering a long and bloody war.

At the very heart of the Christian story is the idea that God sent his Son to earth. But why is this so important? Why was it necessary for God's Son to come to live and die in human history? Could there not have been another way?

Of all the gifts that God gives to his creatures, the most precious and important one is the gift of his Son. In giving his Son, God in effect gave himself, and we need to try to work out why this was the greatest expression of love for the world.

God came himself

If you want a job done well, do it yourself.

I think many of us will have heard this saying, although no-one knows who said it first. Historians have often attributed it to Napoleon, perhaps as he was heading off to Waterloo. Perhaps the sentiment resonates with you or you know someone who lives by that mantra. Funnily enough, it's not something people tend to say when it comes to dentistry or brain surgery (apart from dentists and brain surgeons, of course).

It raises two interesting questions: what are the things we can do for ourselves and what are those we can't? Most of us could follow the route of a canal. But very few of us could do a root-canal.

Throughout the first part of the Bible (the Old Testament), God had called people to relationship with himself. Many times, those people had drifted from him, worshipped false gods and mistreated one another. Often and in various ways, God had called them back to himself. Sometimes, the people would return for a while, but they always returned to their old ways.

Ultimately, God knew that he would have to come himself to deal with the problem of our wayward hearts. It was God – the Son – who came to rescue us from the consequences of our rebellion against God.

Here are five reasons why God had to send his Son.

1 Only Jesus could fulfil the ancient promises

Throughout the Bible, there had been many predictions that one day a saviour would appear to rescue humanity from its mess:

- At the start of the Bible, immediately after humans first rebelled against God, he promised that one of their descendants would come and defeat evil (Genesis 3:15).
- The Old Testament psalms speak of one who would bring salvation. His hands and feet would be pierced, and his clothes would be divided (Psalm 22:16, 18).
- The Old Testament prophets spoke of a saviour who would be born in Bethlehem (Micah 5:2), perform miraculous healings (Isaiah 35:5–6), enter Jerusalem riding on a donkey's colt (Zechariah 9:9), bear and be punished for the sins of all people (Isaiah 53:6), and raised to life after dying (Isaiah 53:11).

These promises are just a few of the many in the Old Testament that refer to the Saviour God promised. All were spoken of hundreds of years before Jesus was born. And yet he fulfilled all the predictions perfectly.

The whole Jewish system of temple, priests and sacrifices enabled people to understand the seriousness of sin and God's holiness. But an animal, however perfect, was never really going to be a proper sacrifice for a human. Jesus came to fulfil the sacrificial system, offering himself as the perfect sacrifice for human sin.

Jesus fulfils the earlier roles that were so important in Israel's life. He's the perfect prophet who speaks truth from God, the perfect priest who brings a once-for-all sacrifice, the perfect king who rules with justice. Jesus is the climax not just of Israel's story but of humanity's story: the one who fulfils Israel's hopes and offers the solution to humankind's deepest needs.

2 Only Jesus could reveal our plight and its solution

A few years ago, my family took a week's holiday in Norfolk. We set off on a Sunday evening and, by the time we arrived, it was dark. We drove around for a long time searching for, before eventually finding, our caravan. We then had to scramble around beneath the caravan, in the dark, to turn on water and gas. It wasn't the most relaxing start. The next morning, as we wandered round the site, we couldn't believe what a meal we'd made of it all. It seemed so straightforward and obvious in the full light of day.

Two of John's favourite images are those of light and darkness. Right at the start of his Gospel account, he says, 'In him [Jesus] was life, and that life was the light of all mankind. The light shines in the darkness, and the darkness has not overcome it' (John 1:4–5). Jesus came to bring light to our darkness. He shone a light over our world. He showed us love. He spoke truth. He did things that amazed those who saw them.

Some people loved it; others hated him for it. His teaching was so controversial that it ended with his own death – *and also* with the birth of the world's largest religion.

Jesus' claims and actions were astonishing. He went around promising forgiveness from God for people's sins. He claimed to be the only way to God. He asked people to leave everything to follow him. These are not the actions of just another teacher. C. S. Lewis said that the sort of things Jesus said and did meant that he was either a liar or a lunatic, or the Lord:

> A man who was merely a man and said the sort of things Jesus said would not be a great moral teacher. He would either be a lunatic – on a level with the man who says he is a poached egg – or else he would be the Devil of Hell. You must make your choice. Either this man was, and is, the Son of God: or else a madman or something worse.[1]

As we read the things Jesus did and said, we have a choice to make. Are we prepared to come into the light or will we retreat into the darkness?

3 Only Jesus could die for our sins

I love a good biography. I can sit for hours reading about the lives of fascinating historical figures. Imagine picking up a modern biography in your favourite book-shop. You get home and sit down in your favourite chair with a good cup of coffee. You flick through the pictures and contents, and you find that the last third of the book is devoted entirely to the events surrounding the person's death. I suspect we'd think the author was weirdly fixated. No Pulitzer Prize there.

Yet all four biographies of Jesus – the New Testament Gospels of Matthew, Mark, Luke and John – give extended space to his death. The entire story builds towards this climactic moment. Jesus himself predicts his own death three times. But it's no accident. He knows exactly what he's doing and where he's going. It's the very reason why he has come.

But why? Why is Jesus' death so important? The answer is in *what his death achieves*. Let's focus on four details in the accounts:

1 *The darkness* (Mark 15:33; Luke 23:44). As Jesus hangs on the cross dying, we are told that darkness comes over the land for three hours. This is more than an eclipse or a gloomy day. People in ancient times knew that this was something extraordinary. In the Old Testament, darkness was a sign of God's judgment. Somehow, in his death, Jesus is bearing God's judgment, even though he's done nothing wrong himself.

2 *Jesus' cry* (Matthew 27:46; Mark 15:34). Jesus cries out, 'My God, my God, why have you forsaken me?' This expresses Jesus' anguish as he experiences some sort of rejection and separation from God the Father.

3 *The temple curtain* (Matthew 27:51; Mark 15:38; Luke 23:45). When Jesus dies, the curtain is torn in two from top to bottom. The temple in Jerusalem

was the place of sacrifice, and God was said symbolically to dwell in the innermost room: the holy of holies. At its entrance was a huge curtain separating it from the rest of the temple. The high priest could enter, only once a year, with a sin offering. The temple curtain was in effect a giant 'stop' sign telling people that they couldn't enter the presence of a holy God. When the curtain was torn, the sacrificial system was ended. Jesus was the ultimate sacrifice. The 'stop' sign was taken away and everyone and anyone could enter God's presence to find forgiveness and friendship with him.

4 *The centurion's cry* (Mark 15:39). The centurion would have been a hardened military man. He'd have seen plenty of people die. But there is something about Jesus' death that catches him by surprise. He can't help but exclaim, 'Surely this man was the Son of God!'

When we put the clues together, we begin to see why Jesus came. He came to live the life of perfect obedience to God that we have not lived and never could live. Then he died to bear the judgment that we deserve because of our sin. As he took that judgment in our place, he made a way for us to receive forgiveness and enjoy a restored relationship with God our maker. The theologian and preacher John Stott wisely said, 'The essence of sin is man substituting himself for God, while the essence of salvation is God substituting himself for man.'[2]

John Stott also tells the story of Father Maximilian Kolbe, a prisoner at Auschwitz. One day, a number of prisoners were selected for execution, including a married man who had children. The man begged for his life. Kolbe volunteered to take the man's place. The officers accepted his offer, and he was placed in an underground cell and left to die of starvation. He sacrificed himself so that another might live. This is what Jesus does for us on the cross. Astonishing. He takes the penalty we deserve so that we can be forgiven.

Only he was worthy, and capable, of restoring human beings to their original God-given dignity. We could never achieve this for ourselves through our own religious or moral effort. It is entirely the gift of the One who loved us enough to give himself for us.

4 Only Jesus could conquer death

My brother and I haven't always got on well. When we were kids, we often squabbled. It's only as we've got older that we've reached the stage at which we really enjoy being together. However, for all his qualities, he wouldn't claim to be perfect. Who would? So if your sibling were to claim to be God, how would you respond? What would it take for you to believe such a crazy claim?

Jesus' story doesn't end in death. Three days later, he rose again and appeared to his followers, and to many others, over a period of several weeks. The evidence for the resurrection is considerable, but I've room only for a few key points here:

- None of Jesus' opponents denied that the tomb was empty.
- The first witnesses were women, in days when a woman's testimony was not considered legally admissible (so this seems an unlikely detail to invent).
- Almost all of Jesus' closest followers died as martyrs, convinced that they'd seen Jesus after he'd come back to life, including his own brother, James. There it is: Jesus' own brother had become so convinced that Jesus was the Son of God that he was prepared to die for that belief.

One early church leader wrote the following: 'After that, [Jesus] appeared to more than five hundred of the brothers and sisters at the same time, most of whom are still living' (1 Corinthians 15:6). In other words, this was evidence that could be corroborated by eyewitnesses at the time of writing. As crazy as a physical resurrection from the dead sounds, the historical evidence is compelling.[3] This resurrection was God's verdict of approval over the work and mission of the Son, whose sacrifice had dealt with our sin and guaranteed us eternal life.

Malcolm Muggeridge was a former BBC journalist who, by the admission of his own family, was far from being a saint. In his later years, he found faith and, according to those closest to him, it profoundly changed him. Shortly before his death, he wrote the following:

Jesus audaciously abolished death, transforming it from a door that slammed to, into one that opened to whoever knocked . . . As I approach my own end, which cannot now be long delayed, I find Jesus' outrageous claim to be, himself, the resurrection and the life, ever more captivating . . . in the limbo between living and dying, as the night clocks tick remorselessly on, and the black sky implacably shows not one single streak or scratch of gray, I hear those words: *I am the resurrection and the life*, and feel myself to be carried along on a great tide of joy and peace.[4]

Jesus conquered the power of death, and he promises that he can take us through that door, too.

5 Only Jesus could give us a truly full life

Have you ever tried cooking a chicken in a dishwasher?

I suspect not. Most of us know the difference between an oven and a dishwasher. But imagine if we didn't and we mixed up the instructions for the two. We'd prep the chicken, potatoes and stuffing, add the seasoning and a bit of butter, and in she goes. We could punch some buttons, return a couple of hours later, and we'd find ourselves opening the door to a hot, wet, inedible mess.[5]

Yet our culture cooks chickens in dishwashers. We have thrown away the Maker's instructions and opted to work it out for ourselves. Consequently, many people look at the results of a life lived without reference to God and find that they've opened the door to chicken gloop or worse.

God isn't out to ruin your life. His words of instruction are for your good and, when you follow them, you find yourself living life in all its fullness. At one point Jesus says, 'I have come that they may have life, and have it to the full' (John 10:10). I suspect that many people think that religion ruins life, that becoming a Christian takes away all the good stuff. But Jesus says, 'Not true.' Actually, when we listen to Jesus, we come to learn more of what it means to be human, to have dignity and purpose and to live in the light of eternal hope. God's plan is for our flourishing. When we keep close to him and his words, we gain a deeper, fuller satisfaction in our lives.

'God did not send his Son into the world to condemn the world, but to save the world through him' (John 3:17). Out of love, God gave the greatest gift to the world: his Son. He came himself – to show us God, to show us ourselves and to show us salvation. Jesus conquered sin and death. He has shown us life to the full. This is the greatest gift ever, anywhere, to anyone. Yet so many will leave the gift unwrapped in the corner, unaware of its true value.

Pick up the gift, check the name label and you'll see who the gift is for . . .

6

That whoever . . .

> For God so loved the world that he gave his one and only Son, **that whoever** believes in him shall not perish but have eternal life.
> (John 3:16)

Weddings are, for the most part, exciting and happy occasions. However, one element that often causes stress is whom to invite. Thankfully, when I got married, those picking up the bill were very generous, and we didn't have any real disagreements about who could and could not come.

But this isn't always the case. Often numbers are limited, and decisions have to be made about who is and who is not invited. Then there's the seating plan: who will sit with whom? Do family members get along or do they need to be kept apart? Throwing a big party sounds like fun, but it can easily become an organizational nightmare, particularly when deciding who *isn't* going to be invited. I know my wife Sarah and I upset at least one person.

Like most people, I like to be invited to things. I don't like the feeling of being rejected or missing out. We call this FOMO: 'fear of missing out'. Being invited makes us feel wanted and valued.

Here, in John 3:16, we see an open invitation. God loves and God gives, and the gift, says John, can be for *whoever*. This is no reluctant invitation just to keep a grumpy aunt happy. Here is a genuine invitation for any and for all, including you.

Several objections come to mind at the idea of God's invitation being for anyone.

Six common objections

Objection 1: 'But I've messed things up too badly!'

In 2017, the former US President Donald Trump announced on Twitter: 'Going to the White House is considered a great honour for a championship team. Stephen Curry is hesitating; therefore, invitation is withdrawn!' The Golden State Warriors had won the US National Basketball Association (NBA) championship, which, traditionally, led to an invitation to the White House to meet the President. Some of the players, including Stephen Curry, were unsure whether they should accept, given that they disagreed with some of Donald Trump's policies. The invitation was withdrawn. The crime of disrespecting the President was, apparently, unforgivable.[1]

We may think that we've done things that would result in God justly revoking his invitation. The weight of guilt from former mistakes can leave us struggling to forgive ourselves. The idea that God could forgive us seems too much.

I love the story of the thief on the cross.[2] As Jesus is being crucified, one of the criminals next to him begins to hurl insults. The other rebukes him: 'Don't you fear God?' And then he turns to Jesus and says, 'Will you remember me when you come into your kingdom?' (Luke 23:40, 42).

In our English versions of the Bible, we read that this man was a criminal or a thief. Many experts think the translation is probably not quite accurate. The Romans generally didn't crucify common criminals or thieves. Crucifixion was the most degrading punishment they had, reserved for the very worst – for rebels or insurrectionists, criminals who had attempted to lead an uprising against the might of Rome. They had to be publicly executed in the most awful, degrading, shameful way possible, as a deterrent to others. So the men crucified next to Jesus were probably not thieves. Today, we might be more likely to call them something far worse – terrorists.

The terrorist turns to Jesus and asks, could someone like you forgive someone like me? I think the first readers of these accounts would have expected rejection or rebuke from the lips of Jesus. Yet Jesus replies, 'Today you will be with me in paradise' (Luke 23:43).

If I'm honest, I'm not sure whether to be amazed at Jesus' powers of forgiveness or offended that these kinds of people seem to be able to get themselves off the hook simply by asking. Is it right or fair? Don't they deserve to be punished for their crimes? How can Jesus simply forgive?

Following the Second World War, Nazi war criminals were sent to Nuremberg to stand trial. They included some of Hitler's closest associates: Hermann Göring, Rudolf Hess and Joachim von Ribbentrop. The US sent two of their own military chaplains, Henry Gerecke and Richard 'Sixtus' O'Connor to offer pastoral care. Understandably, this was not an easy or lightly taken assignment. Gerecke was 52 and two of his own sons were in the forces. Both men received hate mail and were called Nazi lovers for accepting the position. In their own minds, they felt obliged to show the love of God even to the worst of criminals.[3]

Gerecke and O'Connor arrived in November 1945. They conducted simple services and spoke with the prisoners. Some were open and interested, while others were hardened and refused to talk. It was eleven months later that the trials were completed and the verdicts given. Gerecke visited those condemned to die on the eve of their execution. Göring was unrepentant, saying, 'I'll take my chances, my own way.' Later that evening, he took his own life with a cyanide capsule. Gerecke was able to speak and pray with others, many of whom had softened to him and his message in the preceding year.

The next morning Joachim von Ribbentrop was first to be taken to the gallows. He'd been convicted as being instrumental in starting the war and planning early invasions in Czechoslovakia and Poland. He'd also been adjudged to have been deeply involved in the Holocaust.

During his months in prison, he'd become increasingly interested in Gerecke's message, talking with Gerecke and attending services.

As von Ribbentrop was led to the gallows, and the noose was placed around his neck, a US officer asked him for any final words. He replied, 'I place all my confidence in the Lamb who made atonement for my sins. May God have mercy on my soul.' He then turned to Gerecke and said, 'I'll see you again.' A hood was then pulled over his head, and the trap door opened.[4]

Can God's gift of forgiveness really be for such a person? This is truly the test case of whether we understand the grace of God in Jesus' death on the cross. If the story of von Ribbentrop offends you, then you haven't yet understood God's grace.

At the cross, sin is not being ignored or remaining unpunished. It is, rather, the case that Jesus is bearing the full weight of punishment that sin deserves – even that due to the very worst of criminals.

If Jesus can forgive the terrorist on the cross, and if God could forgive someone like von Ribbentrop, he can forgive you. It is impossible for you to have messed up to the degree where you are beyond God's grace. Our sin, however bad, never revokes God's invitation.

Objection 2: 'But I'm not good enough! Why would God want me?'

A recent study published in the *Lancet Psychiatry* journal found that issues related to self-esteem, body image and social anxiety are rising sharply among the younger generation.[5] In England, up to one in five women, aged between 16 and 24, had self-harmed as a way of dealing with mental and emotional distress. Self-harm across the sexes and age groups has risen dramatically in the past twenty years. One expert links these anxieties to 'exam pressures, bullying using social media, and increasing concerns over body image'.[6]

We might not consider ourselves too evil for God's acceptance, but we might wonder if we're good *enough*. Would God really want to know us and relate to us? When it comes to God, faith or church, we may struggle with what has been termed 'imposter syndrome': the fear of being exposed as a fraud. We may be able to put on a good face in front of others but fear that, in the presence of an all-knowing God, our inadequacies would be painfully exposed.

In Roald Dahl's classic story, *Charlie and the Chocolate Factory*, a group of children and their parents are given a tour of Willy Wonka's magical chocolate factory. Mr Wonka takes the children to see the nut room, in which a hundred squirrels are shelling walnuts. They tap each nut, discarding the bad. A spoiled child named Veruca Salt demands that her father buys her one of the squirrels. Mr Wonka replies that they are not for sale, at which point Veruca enters the nut room to attempt to take one for herself. As soon as she enters, the squirrels surround her, pin her down, and one begins tapping her head with his knuckles. At once, the squirrels pick her up and drag her towards the rubbish chute, as Mr Wonka exclaims, 'My goodness, she *is* a bad nut after all . . . Her head must have sounded quite hollow.'[7]

Perhaps that's how you think God views you? Are you afraid that he might discard you as a bad nut, so to speak? But John says, 'God so loved the world that he gave his only son, that *whoever*.'

Elsewhere Jesus said, 'Come to me, all you who are weary and burdened, and I will give you rest' (Matthew 11:28), and that 'whoever comes to me I will never drive away' (John 6:37). It's not 'come to me' if you are good enough or sorry enough, or if you're prepared to try hard enough. It's not 'some' or 'most' who 'come to me'. It's an invitation, a promise. Come – *whoever* – he will welcome you, and he will never drive you away from his presence.

Objection 3: 'But I've never been religious or churchy.'

'Fake it till you make it' is the mantra. I was 17, standing in the nightclub queue – heart pounding, mouth dry, stomach churning, clutching my fake ID – hoping to make it past the security guys on the door. I was sure they would see through the dodgy ID, see through me. I was 17 but looked 15. How would I ever fake my way through?

Sometimes, people aren't so much scared of God as scared of religion or church. They think that to have faith means behaving in certain religious ways in certain religious places or contexts. We can feel like imposters in unfamiliar environments, trying to 'fake' our way through. If you've never really attended church, it can be easy to reject God completely. After all, if faith requires me to attend boring services and hang out with boring, judgmental people, perhaps I'm better off without it?

A while ago, I wanted to do something to experience what it was like for an outsider to walk into a strange place. So I went to a betting shop. Now, I'd never set foot in a betting shop in my life. And this one had no windows to see into, and its door was covered with graphics. As I walked in, I could sense people staring. I knew they knew that I didn't belong. And now what? Where was I to turn? Where was I to go? What was I to do? I went to the corner and found a slip, but it was utterly confusing. There were so many boxes to tick. At last, I worked it out and placed my 50p bet on the result of a football match. As I approached the counter, I could feel my heart racing. I handed the betting slip over to the spotty youth on the other side. He looked at me, knowing as well as everyone else that I was an imposter. He amended my slip because I'd managed to complete it incorrectly, and took my 50p. I stood there waiting to be dismissed. Eventually, I left the shop and couldn't believe how stressful the experience had been. I think I actually won my bet but there was no way I was ever going back to find out.

Walking into a church building can seem like that for some. It can be every bit as nerve-wracking as it was for me to walk into the betting shop. I know of one guy who sat outside in his car, watching people coming in and out of church, for several Sundays before he felt brave enough to come through the door himself.

I can understand that. I recently joined a running club. It was even more anxiety-inducing than I'd anticipated. I didn't go along for ages. I followed their Facebook group, watched their meeting schedule and read the comments from a safe distance. Eventually, I plucked up the courage to join the other runners, and it was great. There was someone to lead the routes and set a pace that I could keep up with, and a group that liked talking about shoe cushioning and arch supports! In the same way, while church can be daunting, there will always be people to help and encourage you if you are a first-timer, just as joining other runners encouraged me with my own running.

Going to church isn't what *makes* you a Christian, however. Sure, it will be helpful. It will also be something you'll hopefully want to do if you decide to find out more. And it really isn't all that scary. But we don't accept God's invitation by doing more religious things. The *whoever* invite doesn't come with the qualification '*whoever* goes to church'. John doesn't say, 'God so loved the world that he gave his one and only Son, that whoever goes to church . . .' Ultimately, going to church doesn't make you a Christian any more than standing in your garage makes you a car. Attending church won't earn you God's approval. But you will find that, as you begin a journey following Jesus, you will *want* to go to church, meet with other Christians, and learn more about God's amazing grace and how to live for him.

Objection 4: 'But I don't think that I know or understand enough.'

Whenever I run discussion groups about exploring the Christian faith, this question regularly surfaces. Many people think that they can't get involved or commit in any sense because there are still things they don't understand or questions with which they're still wrestling. My response is always the same: it is fine to be a follower of Christ who's still working through doubts and questions. There will always be more to learn and things we don't fully understand.

All Souls College in Oxford has a notoriously difficult exam for those applying for a Fellowship. It involves four separate three-hour papers. Two will be on your specialist subject, while the other two will be general. The questions are often abstract, so there are no right or wrong answers. Until recently, there was also a fifth paper that contained just a single word on which the candidate had to write an essay. Often, as many as eighty of the very brightest and best apply; only one or two make the cut.

You'll know by now that Christianity is not like that. There are no exam papers, no trick questions and no pass or fail mark. God's gift and invitation are for all, regardless of how much or how little you know or understand about Christianity or the Bible. I know many people who have been followers of Jesus Christ for longer than I've been alive, and they still have questions. That's OK – even good! The most common word Jesus used for his followers was 'disciples', which could be

translated 'learners'. We're all lifelong learners of what
it means to be followers of Jesus Christ.

Objection 5: 'But I don't know what I'm supposed to *do* with this God stuff.'

I remember a discussion group in my home one evening.
A woman said, 'I think I understand what you're saying
about God's gift, but I don't know what I'm supposed to
do with all this.' She thought there was still something
she had to *do* in response to receiving the gift, whether
it was attending church, reading her Bible and praying,
telling others about her faith or giving money to charity.
Of course, all these things are good; they often flow out
of a heart that has been touched by God's grace and
kindness. However, it is important to say that none of
this *doing* is integral to receiving the gift. Remember the
terrorist on the cross? Nothing he could do would either
earn or repay the gift that Jesus was offering. He simply
asked and received with his dying breath.

When I was younger, someone helpfully used an
illustration of a train, with its engine and coaches. God's
grace is the engine that pulls everything behind. What
follows (the coaches) are the increased love, knowledge,
obedience, service, works and everything else.

Religious ways of thinking can put things the other
way around. I often slip into thinking that it is my
effort and my good works that are the engine. As a
consequence, it seems as if the gift of grace follows after-
wards, that it is a reward for my moral effort. Yet the
Bible is clear that God's gift is not dependent on my

moral or spiritual efforts. My response to God's grace is just that – a *response* to what he has already done for me.

All this is really a way of trying to say that you don't have to *do* anything. God loved the world and he gave the gift of his Son for whoever. It is a gift to be received, not a status to be achieved.

Objection 6: 'But what if it's all too good to be true?'

What if Christianity is a spaghetti tree?

In 1957, the BBC TV programme *Panorama* began a broadcast with these words:

> Here in the Ticino, on the borders of Switzerland and Italy, the slopes overlooking Lake Lugano have already burst into flower, at least a fortnight earlier than usual. But what, you may ask, has the early and welcome arrival of bees and blossom to do with food? Well, it's simply that the past winter, one of the mildest in living memory, has had its effect in other ways as well. Most important of all, it's resulted in an exceptionally heavy spaghetti crop.[8]

Obviously, it was a prank, but that did not stop hundreds of Brits, unfamiliar with the origins of this strange Italian food, phoning in to ask how they might grow their own spaghetti trees.

Is this invitation all too good to be true? Is all this talk of grace the spiritual equivalent of the spaghetti tree?

I often get emails purporting to be from HMRC, informing me of a tax rebate. All I have to do is accept the invitation to hand over my bank details and they'll do the rest. Thankfully, I know that these emails *are* too good to be true.

Is the message of Christianity the greatest and cruellest trick ever played on humanity?

This isn't the place to do a deep dive into all the historical evidence for Christianity. (There are lots of places where you could go to find out more.[9]) Suffice to say that there is exceptionally good evidence for the reliability of the documents that make up the Bible. Wider archaeological evidence, too, supports its claims. You can find historical evidence for the resurrection of Jesus Christ, some of which we touched on earlier. I've spent a considerable amount of my adult life considering the various strands of evidence for Christianity. I am convinced that it is no grand deception but, rather, comprises true accounts and true claims with the power to transform lives.

Every summer the Queen hosts three garden parties at Buckingham Palace. These are a way of recognizing and rewarding public service. Guests cannot apply to attend or invite themselves. They must be nominated by someone and then considered. Where I live, nominations must be sent to the Lord-Lieutenant of Bedfordshire. Those nominated must be British or Commonwealth citizens, and a reason for their nomination must be supplied. I'm not holding my breath for an invitation any time soon.

The invitation John speaks of, by contrast, requires no test of citizenship, no nomination and no consideration by others. There is no panel of judges deciding your fate. It is an open invitation: a gift for *whoever*.

So much of religion can be like the US health-care system. Christianity is more like the UK health-care system. In the USA, you have to pay into a medical insurance plan if you want to receive treatment. In the UK, care is free at the point of access to whoever needs it, regardless of wealth or status. Christianity does not require you to put significant deposits into the religious insurance programme of heaven. God's gift of grace, as we've seen, is free to all who wish to come and receive.

Whoever is John's claim. *Whoever* is Jesus' call.

7

Believes . . .

For God so loved the world that he gave his one
and only Son, that whoever **believes** in him shall
not perish but have eternal life.
(John 3:16)

'Make a wish,' they said. The birthday cake was in front
of me. The candles had just been blown out. Relatives
butchered a rendition of 'Happy birthday'. And then my
mum said, 'Make a wish.'

I expect many of us remember doing something
similar when we were children. There were, of course,
conditions attached. First, you weren't allowed to
tell anyone what you'd wished for or it wouldn't come
true. Second, you had to believe with all your heart.
One birthday, I closed my eyes, blew out the candles
and wished for a new bike. I didn't tell anyone, and I
believed with all the belief I could muster. Guess what?
No bike.

Is that what is meant by faith? Closing our eyes and
believing with all our hearts, only to be disappointed?
Belief is not wishful thinking that ends in disappointment. Belief (or faith) is something we exercise all the
time; it's a crucial part of what it means to be a Christ
follower.

John says that the message about God's love for the world, in sending his Son Jesus, is not something merely to be heard or repeated, but something to be believed: 'For God so loved the world that he gave his one and only Son, that whoever *believes* . . .'

What belief is not

Unhelpful ideas about its nature often hinder our faith. Here are four misunderstandings.

Misunderstanding 1: belief as 'wishful thinking'

'I believe. I believe. It's silly but I believe,' repeats Susan, the little girl in the Christmas film *Miracle on 34th Street*, as she hopes against hope that Santa is real and will grant her Christmas wish.[1]

Faith or belief is often set against reason. Belief, it is claimed, is naive, superstitious, unenlightened and ignorant. Reason, on the other hand, is concerned with evidence, facts, data and proof. Faith is a leap in the dark; reason turns on the light. Or so it is claimed.

The atheist Bertrand Russell wrote:

We may define 'faith' as a firm belief in something for which there is no evidence. Where there is evidence, no one speaks of 'faith'. We do not speak of faith that two and two are four or that the earth is round. We only speak of faith when we wish to substitute emotion for evidence.[2]

Another atheist, Sam Harris, wrote, 'It is time we admitted that faith is nothing more than the license religious people give one another to keep believing when reasons fail.'[3] Or, to put it even more forcefully, here is A. C. Grayling: 'Faith is a commitment to belief contrary to evidence and reason.'[4]

Each of these writers expresses the view that faith flies in the face of facts. Faith, they say, is not interested in evidence and, sometimes, it will even operate contrary to evidence. These are significant claims, which would be disturbing if true.

However, Christianity is not a religion that encourages its followers to ignore reason or evidence. The Christian philosopher J. P. Moreland says, 'It is a great misunderstanding of faith to oppose it to reason or knowledge . . . In actual fact, faith – confidence, trust – is rooted in knowledge.'[5] Elsewhere, he defines faith as 'a trust in and commitment to what we have reason to believe is true'.[6] Faith is not baseless but puts its trust in that which is reasonable and trustworthy.

The biblical writers themselves appealed to reason and proof as they recorded historical events. When the writer Luke recorded his account of Jesus' life, he opened by saying, 'I myself have carefully investigated everything from the beginning' (Luke 1:3). He has used various sources of evidence and invites scrutiny. John, too, in his account of Jesus' life, described how he'd recorded things done in the presence of eyewitnesses so that people might believe what was claimed.[7] When Paul described how more than five hundred people had been eyewitnesses to Jesus' resurrection, he went on to say that many of those people were still alive. Anyone could check the evidence for themselves.[8] As Paul stood trial before Roman rulers, he stated that none of 'it was . . . done in a corner', referring to the events surrounding the life and death of Jesus and his followers.[9] There are eyewitnesses, written records and verbal reports. All of this is hard evidence with which to grapple and engage.

Christianity does not ask us to believe contrary to evidence and reason. Rather, Christianity invites us to examine the historical evidence and the written accounts, and to believe the findings based on good evidence and sound reason.

Misunderstanding 2: belief as a 'fuzzy feeling'

Sometimes, people have somewhat mystical notions of faith, tying it to emotional experiences or feelings. In this case, faith is only as strong as my current feelings; it can come and go.

Again, this is not how the Bible understands faith. It isn't that our emotions are unimportant; rather, emotion is not the basis for what we decide to put our trust in.

In *Mere Christianity*, C. S. Lewis has two helpful chapters on the nature of faith. He opens one by noticing how emotion often runs contrary to our beliefs. He gives the example of undergoing an operation. Our faith in the surgeon is rooted in the knowledge that he has received the necessary training and is qualified to perform the surgery. We trust that the surgeon won't start cutting us open until the anaesthetist has successfully rendered us unconscious. But, says Lewis, 'that does not alter the fact that, when they have me down on the table and clap their horrible mask over my face, a mere childish panic begins inside me'.[10]

In this instance, it isn't that we've lost faith. Our faith is reasonably placed in our knowledge of all the facts to hand. The problem is that emotion has taken over.

Lewis says of faith that it is

the art of holding onto things your reason has once accepted, in spite of your changing moods . . . unless you teach your moods 'where to get off', you can never be a sound Christian or even a sound atheist, but just a creature dithering to and fro, with its beliefs really dependent on the weather and the state of its digestion.[11]

Belief is not the absence of feeling and emotion, but those things do have to be grounded in historical reality.

Misunderstanding 3: belief as *merely* intellectual assent

Jess stands in the window of the burning building, and the firefighter calls out to her to jump. She can't remain where she is but she's too terrified to leap. She knows the firefighter is there; she can hear his voice. But the exercise of faith requires more. Jess needs to trust that voice and make the leap. Fast!

Having seen that belief is not ignorant superstition, we should note that it is not *merely* intellectual assent.

Belief requires more than just agreement with a set of facts.

We believe or trust all sorts of things all the time. Every time you sit on a chair, you trust it won't collapse. Every time you eat in a restaurant, you trust that the food is thoroughly cooked. Every time you catch a bus, you trust the driver to have a licence. Every time you put your credit card details into a website, you trust you're not being scammed. These actions don't require long hours of soul-searching to arrive at the point of faith. Often, we exercise faith without even thinking.

It is, of course, true that as the stakes increase, so too does the process of belief. You would not agree to marry a person while knowing next to nothing about him or her. You wouldn't purchase a house without making several important investigations. Ultimately – even after the passing of time, with greater knowledge and the completion of reasonable checks – there will be a commitment involved that goes beyond a mere intellectual decision.

Belief, as described in the Bible, similarly requires a commitment, not so much to a set of abstract truths but to a person, Jesus Christ. That commitment is not merely intellectual but must also involve the will and the emotions.

Misunderstanding 4: belief as the absence of questions or doubts

Tom, one of my former teachers, died young. He was taken suddenly, in the prime of his life and work. Many of us wondered why God had taken away this man – husband, father, friend, mentor – far too soon.

Faith is not the absence of questions or doubts, as we noted earlier. In fact, if there were no questions or doubts, faith would be unnecessary. Faith is a conscious commitment even in the continuing presence of some questions or doubts. We see this even in the Bible. One of the prophets in Israel, who lived about two and half thousand years ago, cried out:

> How long, LORD, must I call for help,
>   but you do not listen?
> Or cry out to you, 'Violence!'
>   but you do not save?
> (Habakkuk 1:2)

Here is one of God's prophets questioning why God didn't seem to be listening to his prayers.

Sometimes, people think that, unless they have 'perfect faith', they can't possibly be ready to step out on the journey of faith. The Bible says, 'Not so.' Jesus himself spoke of faith as small as a mustard seed. Of course, it requires belief, trust and commitment, but it also recognizes the reality of our humanness, our questions and struggles. Sometimes, surprisingly, these things make more sense *once* we've stepped out on the journey. As the writer G. K. Chesterton once said, 'The riddles of God are more satisfying than the solutions of man.'[12] In other words, sometimes it's better to confess that we don't understand everything about

God than to pretend that we, as humans, have all the answers.

If you're putting off that initial step of faith until you've got all the answers to your questions, then you'll be waiting for ever. Faith, I reiterate, is not the absence of questions and doubt.

So, now that we've outlined what faith is *not*, what can we say positively about the nature of 'belief'?

What belief is

Christians down through the ages have generally recognized three elements of belief or faith: understanding, assent and trust. Each is necessary for a proper grasp of what it means to believe.

1 Understanding

There must be a basic understanding of what the Christian faith is about. If, after reading this book, you think Christianity is about rule-keeping and being nice, then I've failed. I'd have left you with a wrong understanding.

Belief requires that we believe *in* something or someone, and we can't believe in something we basically don't understand. As we've seen so far, in considering John 3:16, some of the basics of the Christian message may be summarized as follows:

- There is a God.
- He loves this world – he's not distant or uncaring.

- The 'world' (including you and me) has rebelled against him, which the Bible calls 'sin'.
- He gave: Christianity is about his grace, not our works.
- His Son: Jesus came to reveal God to us, to show us what we're like and, ultimately, to die in our place, taking the punishment that our rebellion deserves.
- Whoever: this message is for all people, not just some people.
- Believes: we can come back to God simply by trusting in what Jesus has done for us.

These are some of the basic truths of Christianity that we need to understand if we are to put our faith in Jesus. However, it's important to emphasize again: this isn't an exam requiring a 'grade A' understanding. There are lots of things that Christians will have questions about.

2 Assent

Belief has within it a sense of assent or agreement. It begins with understanding the claims, then moves to a point of agreement with those claims. I *understand* that some people think mushrooms taste good; I just don't agree. No-one should eat fungus. It's an abomination.

Recently, I saw a documentary about a group of people who believe that the earth is flat. I'm not quite sure why I watched it – a sort of morbid curiosity, perhaps. Flat-earthers write books, host online video lectures and organize annual conferences. As I watched,

I was fascinated with the theories presented and the attempts to counter the mainstream view of the earth as a sphere. I wouldn't claim fully to understand everything that they've written, but I think I grasped enough of the basics to understand the claim. However, I disagree with the claim. Their evidence is ultimately unpersuasive, and they fail to address the wealth of evidence demonstrating that the earth is a globe, orbiting the sun. So I don't believe the earth is flat. I *understand* the argument but I don't *assent* to it.

I have claimed the Bible teaches that there is one God, that we have all lived lives that dismiss him, that he sent his Son to die for us, and that we can be forgiven through the Son's death on the cross. Belief would not only understand those things but would also agree. Unbelief might understand the claim but would simply not agree that those claims are true.

So there's an element of invitation here. An important question is: 'Do you understand the argument so far?' A *more* important question is: 'Do you agree?'

3 Trust

Belief or faith requires trust. It is one thing to understand and agree. It is another to trust those things for oneself.

Every year our church family takes a group of young people away for a week in the Lake District. Activities include walking, canoeing, climbing and abseiling (rappelling). I'm not particularly fond of heights, so the climbing and abseiling are not my favourites.

When it comes to abseiling, I'm happy with the first two elements of belief. I understand that the rope can take my weight and it's been set up by a competent instructor. I mentally assent to the truth of those things. I've seen other people abseil safely. It's the third element that I struggle with – leaning back on the rope and stepping backwards off the edge. Mentally, I understand and agree. But that isn't enough. It requires trust to commit.

At this point, you may understand how Jesus' death pays the price for your wrongdoing. You may agree that those things happened as recorded. Eventually, though, you have to lean on that for yourself.

Suppose you were planning a day trip to London but weren't sure how to get there. I could tell you that you can catch a train from a certain station, at a certain time, for a certain price. So far, all I have done is simply communicated information to you; you must decide what to do with it.

The first element of belief would require you to have understood me correctly. Are we clear about the location of the station? Did I explain 'peak' and 'off-peak' train times adequately? Did I say the cost was £15 or £50? The second and third elements of faith depend upon a sound understanding of the basic facts.

The second element of faith requires you to consider the truthfulness of the information. Everyone has a friend who thinks he or she knows everything about everything. If that person were to tell us that the best way to get to London was to catch a certain train, at a certain time, for a certain price, we might instinctively be suspicious, wondering whether the information is correct.

If you decide that I'm telling you the truth, it involves the third element of faith: trust. You would have to decide whether or not to act on my information, trusting that I have told you the truth. You would decide whether to make your way to the station, at a certain time, expecting to pay a certain fare. Alternatively, you might decide to listen to someone else and make other plans.

Belief or faith involves an understanding of the message, assent to its truthfulness and then a commitment to trust. It's not about fuzzy feelings or perfect understanding. It's a commitment to begin a journey, with a single step, trusting the message and promise of Jesus Christ.

Of course, you also have to want to take that step. The abseiler translates trust into action when she decides that the experience outweighs the nerves. The bungee jumper leaps because he believes it will offer a new thrill. Are they anxious and unsure? Most are. But for them, the sensation is worth the leap.

'Surely,' you ask, 'there is something I must do?' No. As we saw, Jesus is crystal clear – all that is required is belief in what he has done.

One of C. S. Lewis's chapters on faith in *Mere Christianity* contains this gem:

> I think everyone who has some vague belief in God, until he becomes a Christian, has the idea

of an exam, or of a bargain in his mind. The first result of real Christianity is to blow that idea into bits . . . God has been waiting for the moment at which you discover that there is no question of earning a pass mark in this exam or putting him in your debt . . . Every faculty you have, your power of thinking or of moving your limbs from moment to moment, is given you by God . . . It is like a small child going to its father and saying, 'Daddy, give me sixpence to buy you a birthday present.' Of course, the father does, and he is pleased with the child's present. It is all very nice and proper, but only an idiot would think that the father is sixpence to the good on the transaction.[13]

Lewis is saying that faith itself is a gift. The fact that you're reading this book, that you have a brain putting the pieces of this puzzle together, that someone has spoken to you about these things, that you perhaps are now disposed to find out more – all of this is, I believe, from God. So even our faith is a gift, a work begun in us by God himself.

John Bunyan's famous *The Pilgrim's Progress* shows us that belief is not just an initiatory act or decision, but a continuing journey of trust and learning. The more we learn, the richer our faith becomes. But it must begin somewhere, with an initial decision of the will to start out on the road of faith.

Shortly, we'll consider what is at stake with regard to our decision to believe, or not believe, but next we'll look at perhaps the two most important little words in John 3:16.

8
In him . . .

For God so loved the world that he gave his one and only Son, that whoever believes **in him** shall not perish but have eternal life.
(John 3:16)

Holidays are meant to be relaxing, right?

A few years ago, my family spent a week in Normandy. It was the first time we'd travelled together abroad. We reached Folkestone, excited and nervous about this new adventure, and drove the car on to one of the massive Channel Tunnel trains. As the train started to move, we entered the darkness and began to wonder at this miracle of engineering and the astonishing mass of water above. The film *Daylight* also ran through our minds.[1] Thirty minutes later we emerged from the darkness into France.

Then our excitement turned to panic. As we drove off the train, up the ramp and on to the roads, there were signs everywhere. Everyone else seemed to know exactly where they were going. I knew that if we picked the wrong road, we'd head in completely the wrong direction. And I had about five seconds to pick my lane. We didn't have a satnav, so we were totally reliant on our map. Let's just say it wasn't the most harmonious or relaxed journey. I'm sure the scenery was beautiful but the atmosphere was tense. Thankfully, we all survived: my wife and I didn't get a divorce and no children were harmed for saying, 'Are we nearly there yet?'

If you've ever had a similar experience, you'll know the stress involved. Whoever said that the journey is more important than the destination hadn't spent five hours in a car with small children.

We're going to see that the journey of faith has a pathway marked out. And that all roads *don't* lead to Rome. This is a difficult claim in our modern world. But, first, it's important for us to consider carefully why John includes the words 'in him'.

Faith needs a map

One of the best-connected Underground stations in London is King's Cross. Whether you're coming from the west, the north, the south or the east of the city, there are several different Tube lines you could take to King's Cross. You might get on the Victoria Line, the Piccadilly Line, the Northern Line, the Hammersmith and City Line or the Circle Line and, if you're travelling in the right direction, you will get to King's Cross.

If you're a keen walker, you may know that there are at least six routes up Wales's highest mountain, Snowdon. Pick whichever one you fancy; they all lead to the top.

Many people think that religion or spirituality works a little like that. We pick our preferred routes and, ultimately, we'll all meet up in the same place. However, the Bible tells us that true faith isn't like choosing a Tube line or a walking route. The way has been marked out for us and we have to stick to the path. Faith requires a map and the traveller needs to stick to the route.

This claim is a crucial one. It's not enough to believe in an abstract God or a God of simply any religion. John says that if you're to believe in God, you must also believe *in him* – the Son that he has given. These two little words are, in some ways, the most important and the most challenging of all. John is clear: it is belief *in him* that is necessary.

This point raises all sorts of other questions. What about people who follow other religions or no religion at all? What about those who never hear the message of Christianity? Are Christians so arrogant as to believe that only they know the way to God?

Before attempting to answer, let's take a step back to think about the possibility of taking a wrong path.

Pick the right route

While it's hard to admit, there are plenty of things we believe and get wrong. There are paths we follow that take us in the wrong direction. We sometimes put our trust in people we shouldn't.

A few years ago, I received a phone call from someone claiming to be from Microsoft. He said that he had discovered a virus on my computer. He talked me through a few processes and seemed to know exactly what he was talking about. At this point, he informed me that he could fix the problem for a fee. Fortunately, something told me this wasn't quite right, but I was a whisker away from giving him my credit card details. I'd been taken in by this guy's technical knowledge and nearly paid the price. I'm sure many of us have similar stories of friends or relatives being scammed by people they chose to trust.

Perhaps you've experienced a breakdown in a personal relationship or even been betrayed by someone you trusted. That person, who you believed would never let you down, turned out to be untrustworthy. Few things are more painful.

More trivially, I used to believe that I could eat anything I wanted and get away with it. Then I turned 30, and my metabolism seemed to slow overnight. I found out within a few months that I could no longer eat anything I desired without consequences.

Whether it's in the realm of personal relationships and business transactions, ideology and values, or something more trivial, I think we would all admit that we don't always pick the correct route. When we stop and think about it, the idea of misplaced faith isn't really that controversial. We can be wrong about things and so can others.

We're encouraged to be respectful and tolerant of viewpoints that differ from our own. This is right and proper in a society that believes in freedom of speech, thought and expression. That said, respect and tolerance don't require us to *agree* with every other belief system. Freedom includes the freedom to disagree. In our modern world, there are lots of people with whom we disagree while defending their right to their point of view.

And, of course, there are some beliefs and viewpoints with which we disagree more strongly. I mentioned earlier a documentary that I'd watched about those who believe the earth is flat. They are free to believe it but I strongly disagree with their belief. There have been (and are), in some places of the world, ideologies with which I strongly disagree. Here, I suspect, we might go further and oppose anything that incites or causes harm. There are limits to freedoms and tolerance.

Although we may struggle with the exclusive claims of Christ, elsewhere we're quite used to excluding points of view with which we strongly disagree, especially if we consider them harmful. We would not tolerate the violent expression of a white supremacist as 'just another path up the mountain'. We wouldn't consider the op-pression of women to be just another point of view. So, while we may dislike the idea of exclusivist beliefs, we're all exclusivists to some degree.

One of those beliefs which you might like to exclude is my belief that the only way to God is through Jesus. You might believe that all religions have parts of the truth. But that then begs the question: how would you ever know?

Look again at the map

In Edinburgh, there is a hill about a mile to the east of the city centre called Arthur's Seat. If you climb the

250 metres to the top, you can see the whole city. From down below, it isn't easy to see how roads, parks and churches connect, but you get the whole picture from Arthur's Seat.

For you to know whether each religion had a part of the truth, you would require the equivalent of Arthur's Seat. You would need the whole picture, access to a map that proved all routes reached the summit. But you don't and you can't. So it is simply an assertion that all religions have some part of the total truth. And it is an assertion that turns out to be arrogant in its own right.

In fact, the lack of evidence for such an assertion makes it *more* arrogant than the Christian claim that Jesus is the only way, truth and life. It pretends to offer love and humility, as it distributes this new map, while offering absolutely no idea of whether the new map leads anywhere at all. It would not be loving for me to give you a map I'd simply made up on the back of an envelope and send you off to get lost in the wilderness. What sounds loving and tolerant would turn out to be an instrument of hurt and harm.

Lesslie Newbigin, a writer and former missionary to India, often came across the 'all roads lead to Rome' reasoning about faith. He wrote the following in response:

There is an appearance of humility in the protest-ation that the truth is much greater than any one of us can grasp, but if this is used to invalidate all claims to discern the truth, it is in fact an arrogant claim to a kind of knowledge which is superior to the knowledge which is available to fallible human beings. We have to ask, 'How do you know that the truth about God is greater than what is revealed to us in Jesus?' . . . What is the vantage ground from which you claim to be able to relativize all the absolute claims? . . . What higher truth do you have?[2]

It isn't that you're inclusive and I'm exclusive. We both have an understanding and a boundary to our inclusivism and exclusivism. We are alike in this respect. Everybody has a set of exclusive beliefs. It's just a question of *which* set to embrace.

The question, then, is really one of evidence and justification for our exclusiveness. On what basis can we say that belief placed here is necessary and that belief placed there is excluded? Ultimately, who says so?

Don't miss the right path

So here's the claim we've been considering: God gave his Son, and belief in him is the key to eternal life. On another occasion, Jesus said, 'I am the way and the truth and the life. No one comes to Father except through me' (John 14:6). That's a pretty exclusive claim. We like to believe that everyone is journeying up the mountain, taking their own paths and that we'll all get to the top eventually. But Jesus says that all the other paths lead to dead ends.

This stance seems intolerant to our modern ears. It strikes us as unloving, arrogant and exclusive. The real question, though, is not how Jesus' claim makes me *feel* but whether he's telling the *truth*. The doctor's diagnosis might upset me but the only question relevant to my future must be: 'Is he right?' The mechanic's verdict (and quote!) may displease me but the only thing that really matters for the safety of my family is whether he's telling the truth. The most important thing is not my feelings on an issue but the truth about that issue.

Was Jesus right to make his claim? If he was, then there is nothing of greater importance for our world.

However, laying it out so starkly is not necessarily going to convince many. We have to examine some evidence for such a claim. Here are just three things that we might consider:

1 Jesus claimed to be God: a claim that ultimately got him killed.
2 Jesus performed miracles, which demonstrated the truth of his claims.
3 Jesus came back to life, further demonstrating the truth of his claims.

But how do we know any of those three happened? Remember some of the evidence we looked at earlier? We have four accounts of the life of Jesus, all written within a generation of the events. Many eyewitnesses were still alive and could quickly have discredited erroneous accounts. The manuscript evidence for these accounts is overwhelming, running into the tens of thousands and demonstrating the reliability of the accounts as we have them. As far as pure history goes, there are few better attested events than Jesus' claims, miracles and resurrection. If he did what he did (and the evidence is incontrovertible), then we must take seriously what he said, including his claims about his own exclusivity as *the* way, truth and life.[3]

We could speculate about those who have never heard, or will never hear, about Jesus and ancient tribal religions that came long before he did, but that's not the issue here. The fact is that *you*, the reader, *have* heard the news about Jesus and his claims. So what will you do with these claims?

The right path is inclusive

Here's one further bold claim: Jesus' exclusive claims are true, and they result in the most loving and inclusive behaviour.[4]

Often, we are told to consider all the ways in which religious views overlap and converge in agreement on various things. Here, I want to consider two ways in which the faith Jesus founded is different, even unique, when compared with other religions.

1 Consider the origin of Jesus' claim

A number of religions claim to be founded on revelation to a human – usually some kind of prophet. Jesus' claim is not that he is merely a prophet; it isn't just that he has heard a message from God. It is that he *is* God. This claim is not only profoundly authoritative; it is more than that.

If God were to humble himself to come down to us in love, what sort of impact would that have on those who followed him? It should result in Christ followers being *more* humble and less arrogant. In the earliest years of Christianity, a radical community of followers arose that welcomed the outcast, the poor, the diseased and the marginalized. In the ancient world, rich and poor didn't mix; Jew and Greek didn't mix; the leprosy sufferer was an outcast. But in the church, they did. The incarnation – God taking on flesh – had modelled a radical sort of humility that Jesus' followers emulated. As Jesus died on the cross, he continued to display love for his enemies. During his greatest humiliation, he modelled the greatest love of all. This gentle humility is the kind that should characterize Jesus' followers, too.

2 Consider the way of salvation

As we noted in earlier chapters, in other religions (such as some from the East), salvation or enlightenment is achieved through a person's own hard work and effort. In Christianity, by contrast, salvation is achieved through God's grace. Jesus lived the perfect life that we are unable to live. He died the death we deserved, in our place, that we might know forgiveness and new life with God. As a result, Christians do not look down on other people, feeling superior in their religious achievement.

Christ followers offer the same grace, mercy, love and humility towards others, whatever their walk of life.

While Jesus' claims are undeniably exclusive, the result is the most inclusive community that there has ever been.

This chapter began with a challenging claim about the exclusivity of faith in Christ. I hope that two things have become apparent:

1 All of us have some sort of exclusivity built into our deepest beliefs and values.
2 The exclusive claims of Jesus are true, and they work themselves out in the most inclusive sorts of behaviour.

But what is at stake concerning our choices about belief?

As it turns out – an awful lot.

9

Shall not perish . . .

> For God so loved the world that he gave his one
> and only Son, that whoever believes in him **shall
> not perish** but have eternal life.
> (John 3:16)

There are few things more feared than 'the talk'. We may
fear heights, snakes or spiders. Many fear the talk more.
You may have it seared into your memory, either as
victim or perpetrator: that parent–child conversation
about the birds and the bees. Some strange folk embrace
the task with gusto (I'm still referring to the talk):
liberal-minded people who are happy to pull out pictures
and props. The rest of us try to avoid this conversation
for as long as possible – sometimes, for ever. A friend of
mine conducted a survey among a class of adult students
asking how many had received the talk from their
parents: 20% were still waiting.

Some topics are difficult to talk about, so we avoid
them. This chapter contains one of them.

The subject of God's final judgment is certainly not
easy to discuss. Many of us would rather avoid it al-
together. Like the talk.

However, sometimes the hardest things to explore are
also the most important. Final judgment is an important

topic, not just because of what is at stake but also because there are so many misunderstandings. Many people think of final judgment as some sort of medieval underground torture chamber, lit with roaring flames and occupied by short, red-horned devils holding pitchforks. Sometimes, it's trivialized or joked about as the place where all the fun people are having a good party. Others simply dismiss the idea as superstitious nonsense used by the church to scare people during the Middle Ages.

All of this has dragged us a long way from Jesus' own teaching on the subject. Many people have never read what Jesus said or are unaware that he said anything at all about final judgment. Sometimes I meet somebody who will say, 'I like Jesus' teaching, but I'm not sure about miracles or the resurrection or his followers.' What they usually mean is that they quite like the bits about turning the other cheek and loving your enemies, which leads me to suspect that they haven't read very much of Jesus' teaching.

Jesus talked about final judgment more than anyone else. He pulled no punches about the final state of those who ultimately decide to reject him. While many non-religious people like bits of what Jesus said, the subject of this chapter is not high up in the 'greatest hits' compilation.

John says, 'God so loved the world that he gave his one and only Son, that whoever believes in him *shall not perish*.' Here, the troubling possibility of 'perishing' for those who choose not to believe is suggested. It raises all sorts of questions. Is God truly loving? What about for-giveness? Isn't this outdated nonsense? Does this really have anything to do with me?

To try to begin to answer some, let's start by remembering the context. John began by saying, 'God so loved the world . . .'

Here's the question: how can a God who loves the world so much condemn people to 'perish'? How can tender love and severe judgment come from the same being?

I want to come at the question from a different angle. In this chapter, I will try to convince you that the concept of judgment *only* makes sense if God is perfectly loving towards his world. I hope to persuade you that judgment is not opposed to love but an expression of perfect love. Below are five ways in which God's judgment manifests, or demonstrates, his love.

Judgment manifesting love

1 Love that's fair

The Great British queue is evidence of an inbuilt sense of justice. We like to line up and wait our turn. Well, we don't like waiting but we like the order and respect involved. No-one is allowed to jump the queue. Whatever your social status, you wait with the rest of us. If someone dares to attempt to cheat, they will be met with a terrifying onslaught of muttering and hard stares. It's not on. It's poor form. It's bad manners. It's just not cricket (whatever that means). The most un-British thing you can do is to queue jump. It's an insult to our deeply felt sense of justice and fair play.

Truth be told, I think that most of us, if we stop to think about it, believe in the ideas of justice and judgment. If we were to take a poll and ask whether Genghis Khan, Adolf Hitler and Joseph Stalin deserved judgment for their crimes, many of us would say yes. Genghis Khan is estimated to have caused the death of forty million people; Stalin, as many as twenty million; Hitler, at least six million. None of these men faced the judgment of a human court. I don't think many of us would object to the idea that they should face judgment for the evil they did. We know from our own lives and media reports that on those occasions when justice fails, it seems to be a betrayal of care for victims and their families.

We saw earlier that sin is a sort of vandalism – more specifically, we could think of it as the vandalism of shalom. The word 'shalom' in the Bible means 'peace', but it also means much more. It speaks of a way of life that brings blessing, flourishing and wholeness.

Humans are naturally good at finding ways to vandalize shalom. Justice is about valuing, upholding and restoring shalom. A lack of justice would be to turn a blind eye to the damage. I hope you are beginning to see that a lack of justice is not at all loving. For God to ignore evil, as if it didn't matter, would not be love; it would be apathetic and uncaring towards the world that he has made, and to the people he made in his image.

If you or I were to run into the National Gallery in London, take out a knife and slash a Rembrandt, that would be an act of vandalism on something beautiful. We would expect to face the consequences. If the authorities simply turned a blind eye or said it didn't matter, something within us would think that was wrong. The vandalism of something lovely, the lack of concern for how our actions affect others and the offence to the artist all require justice. Love for beauty, love for shalom, demands proper justice in the face of vandalism.

In *Why I'm No Longer Talking to White People about Race*, Reni Eddo-Lodge encourages readers to be angry about injustice.[1] There is a sort of anger that can be righteous in the face of injustice. We don't always get these things right, but I think we can agree that there are some things about which anger is indeed right and just.

Justice is not opposed to love; it is a manifestation of a deep love for something that truly matters.

2 Love that protects

Judgment is also the display of protective love for something or someone.

A friend of mine had a child who was being bullied at school. Despite several complaints, calls and meetings, the school failed to deal properly with the situation. Ultimately, the boy's parents had to move him to a different school.

Is judgment in this case harsh, unkind or uncaring? Or does it exhibit a proper concern for the protection of the victim? I suspect that the school staff believed they were showing love, patience, care and gentleness to the offender, but their lack of action was not loving to the victim. In fact, they failed to love both.

Many of you will exercise similar forms of loving protection all the time. If you like to bleach your toilet, you are involved in the mass termination of living organisms – bacteria – for the protection of your family. Your actions might be viewed as barbaric, even maniacal, from the viewpoint of the bacteria. From your perspective, though, you are protecting your family from something that may bring harm, because you love them.

But don't mishear me. I'm not likening people to bacteria! I'm just illustrating that love seeks to protect from harm.

If our homes were broken into in the middle of the night, I expect many of us would do whatever was necessary to protect our loved ones. We would not consider it judgmental or harsh to deal with the threat; it would simply be the natural expression of protective love.

When we discipline our children, we do it sometimes to protect others (a sibling, for example), but also to protect them from becoming adults who will mistreat others. We exercise some form of judgment precisely because we love them so much.

When it comes to God's creation, and its inhabitants, God is fiercely protective. When it comes to God's *new* creation – the new heaven and earth for our eternal enjoyment – he will not let in anything that may spoil or endanger it. All evil and sin will be kept out and far away.

As one writer vividly puts it:

There will be no barbed wire in the kingdom of God . . . For 'barbed wire', of course, read whichever catalogue of awfulness you prefer: genocide, nuclear bombs, child prostitution, the arrogance of empire, the commodification of souls, the idolization of race.[2]

In the future that God has planned, there will be the 'elimination of all that distorts God's good and lovely creation'.[3]

Again, God's judgment is not opposed to his love – it is an expression of his love.

3 Love that respects

One of the mysteries of the Bible is the whole area of free will. Scholars down the ages have wrestled with how to understand the relationship between an all-knowing, all-powerful God and the free agency of human persons.

We might ask, 'If we risk spoiling God's new creation, why doesn't God just transform us all instantly? Wouldn't that be the most loving thing to do?' If even our faith is a gift from God, why doesn't he simply give it to all in the same way?

While the Bible teaches that God is in control, it is also clear that human beings are not puppets or robots, crudely controlled by a divine puppet master. Humans are held responsible and accountable by God for their actions throughout the Bible. God appeals to human beings to return to him. He hears and responds to their prayers when they do.

This area of theology is complex, and I can't provide an easy answer here. I simply want to observe and uphold the mystery. God is truly all-knowing and all-powerful, *and* humans are responsible moral agents, held accountable for their choices. Upholding the mystery means there is truth in the idea that our human choices are real choices invested with inherent dignity.

If we turn our backs on God, saying, in effect, 'My will be done,' there will come a time when God ultimately replies, 'OK, your will be done.' We will be left to face an eternity without him, based on our choice to reject him in this life.

In *A Brave New World*, Aldous Huxley's famous novel, a government attempts to create a society of perfect happiness. Babies are engineered through artificial wombs and indoctrinated as children into certain predetermined classes. A mind-controlling drug, 'soma', is freely given to all to keep them in a state of perpetual happiness. Anybody who behaves or thinks differently from the state's dictated norms is ostracized. After an encounter with a free, 'savage' people, two characters struggle to return to the heavily controlled state. The book finishes with a riot and a suicide. Huxley is showing us that any attempt to make people happy through control or coercion is doomed to failure.[4]

Love does not seek to coerce or manipulate. Human attempts to control are rightly seen as abusive and unloving. A mother knows that she cannot live her child's life for her. Her love will mean recognizing the child's choices, even when it breaks her heart and brings dire consequences. As strange as it sounds, I think it is true to say that there is a sense in which God's love upholds our moral agency, even when it brings us harm.

4 Love that warns

It is important to recognize that warnings about judgment are, in themselves, acts of love. When I tell my children not to run into the road, it isn't because I hate them but because I love them. If a friend were swimming in the sea and we saw a sign warning of sharks, it would be unloving simply to let him or her get on with it. Even the many health warnings in everyday life are rooted in a concern for well-being. Sadly, though, it is true to say that many modern health warnings are given for the supplier's own defence against legal action. Properly conceived, however, they *should* arise from a genuine concern for others.

We tend to think of those passages in the Bible that speak of warning as unloving and harsh. We wish they weren't there. Why can't we just focus on the bits about love and peace and forgiveness? However, if Jesus' teaching about judgment is true, then it is because of Jesus' great *love* for humanity that he speaks so much about judgment. It would be unloving to fail to warn someone of impending danger. Only if Jesus' teaching about judgment were *untrue* would it be unloving and unkind to speak about the subject.

In all of this, we must acknowledge that sometimes Christians have failed and spoken of God's judgment in ways that have been harsh, unkind and uncaring. Yet this failure to speak with love and sensitivity does not mean that the subject is untrue or should be off limits. Jesus' teaching about judgment is like a lighthouse designed to keep you off the rocks.

Warnings are words of love in a minor key, but no less loving for that.

5 Love that pays

A few years ago, I had my car clamped. I felt so silly. I'd parked in a private car park and hadn't stopped to read the signs properly. I thought it'd be OK. I was visiting someone for only a few moments, after all, but it was long enough for someone to turn up, stick a massive yellow Denver boot on my front wheel and issue me with a £120 fine to get it released.

I was gutted. Sarah and I didn't have much money, so it really stung. I was retelling my tale of woe to a friend, and the next day he gave us £120 to cover the loss. I was blown away. It was my mistake, not his. But because he loved us, he wanted to pay the penalty. It was an amazing kindness.

When we think of God's judgment, we must also remember that God so loved the world that he sent his Son. He sent him to die on a cross to take the judgment we deserved. God's love for us is so great that he is prepared to pay the price himself so we don't have to. For those who have faith in Christ, all the judgment originally reserved for us is laid on him. This is how much God loves us, and these are the lengths to which he goes to rescue us.

When we talk about judgment in these terms – as a manifestation of love – I think most of us can understand a little better why it is important and necessary.

Our personal struggle with judgment

Our real struggle with judgment is not with the idea *in principle*, but rather with the idea that God's judgment might have something to do with us personally. We can understand, even applaud, the idea that judgment is a just and protective manifestation of love. We see how evil must be fully eliminated in God's new creation. But we struggle with evil and judgment up close.

In the TV show *The Good Place*, people are sent either to the good place or the bad place, based on a calculation of how much good versus how much evil they've done during their lives on earth. Only about one in a thousand people are good enough for the good place; everyone else goes to the bad place. The main character protests that it is unfair. She acknowledges she's not been perfect but neither has she been evil. At one point she says, 'There should be a medium place for medium people.'[5] I guess that sums up what many people think.

This view fails, however, to recognize the seriousness of sin and evil in our world and in our hearts. The problem is summed up in a famous quote of Aleksandr Solzhenitsyn: 'If only there were evil people somewhere insidiously committing evil deeds, and it were necessary only to separate them from the rest of us and destroy them. But the line dividing good and evil cuts through the heart of every human being.'[6]

We are like people set up for a day on the beach. We've put up our windbreak and laid out our towels. We've made a sandcastle and our picnic basket is open on the rug. The tide is a good way out, so we feel content with our spot. As the day goes on, the tide begins to come in; it gets closer and closer. We begin to wonder whether we have indeed picked the right spot and whether we should move. We think we're safe by our own reckoning but, as we learn more about ourselves and more about a holy God, we begin to recognize that the tide draws ever closer.

My kids enjoy watching *Police Interceptors*, a TV show that follows police pursuit drivers as they track down and tackle crime on the roads, including everything from drunk driving to theft and driving without insurance.[7] In one episode, a young man is stopped in the early hours. He sits in the back of the police car. The officer asks if he's had a drink, to which he replies that he hasn't had a drink at all that day. The police officer presses him a little harder: 'Are you sure you haven't had a drink, because I think I can smell alcohol on you.' The young man replies, 'No, officer. I swear, I haven't had a drink at all today.' Cue the breathalyser and, sure enough, the young man is found to be far above the legal limit and is immediately arrested. It begs the question: why maintain the lie? If the officer has the equipment to prove that you're over the limit one way or the other, why pretend you haven't had a drink?

Similarly, we live our lives before the gaze of an all-knowing Creator. He knows everything we've ever said, thought or done. He knows the things we've done that we shouldn't have done. He knows the things we should have done but didn't do. No part of our lives has ever been hidden from his sight. He knows our motives and the things we've thought about others but would never say out loud. He knows the attitudes of our hearts towards him.

There is an occasion, later in John's account of Jesus' life, on which Jesus comes across a group of men about to stone to death a woman who has been caught in adultery. Jesus says to them, 'Let him who is without sin cast the first stone.'[8] What? They drop their rocks, turn around and walk home with his words ringing in their ears. On another occasion, Jesus says to his hearers, 'Remove the plank from your own eye before taking the speck out of your brother's.'[9] These stories resonate powerfully with us because they reveal our true attitudes.

Can any one of us really stand before the perfect judge and try to plead not guilty? Justice means God can't turn a blind eye to some sins and punish others. If we were to try to keep a record of all the ways that – hour by hour, day by day, week by week, month by month, year by year, decade by decade – we have lived contrary to God's perfect standard of love, goodness and holiness, we couldn't possibly begin to imagine all the ways in which we bear guilt before his majesty.

We need to be honest enough to see sin for what it is. We either come to Jesus and ask him to pay for our sin or we determine that we will pay for it ourselves.

This moment isn't meant to be an introspective one of self-loathing; it is meant to help us to see with realism and honesty the depth of the human problem. There are times in the Bible when people catch a glimpse of God's holiness and fall face down, crying out, 'Woe is me.'[10]

Often, we relativize good and evil according to our own human standards. But that's the wrong scale. It's not enough to say I'm better than them or not as bad as them. The scale belongs to God. It's when we measure ourselves against his perfect holiness that we see how far short we fall. It's not an easy thing to face or admit, but it's crucial that we understand how bad the bad news is if we're to see how good the good news is.

God isn't out to get us, but the weight of waywardness within us has to be removed if we are to spend eternity in his presence. We can't take our mess with us, for it would spoil God's perfect new heaven and new earth. It must be taken and hurled into the depths of the sea.

The truth is that we simply don't like the verdict and we question the right of the judge to come to such a verdict. We think that our own verdict is correct. Everyone else thinks the same. The question is not so much about whether we like the verdict but whether the judge is correct and has the right to dispense the verdict.

Of course, as we've seen, God does not want anyone to perish but for everyone to come to eternal life. He loved the world and he gave his Son, so that whoever believes will not perish. Judgment can be avoided if we come to Jesus in faith and trust that he has borne that judgment for us.

The end of the story for us in this life then becomes the beginning of an incredible story. And it's a story that gets better with every subsequent page.

10

But have eternal life

For God so loved the world that he gave his one and only Son, that whoever believes in him shall not perish **but have eternal life**.
(John 3:16)

The first funeral I ever took was for Samuel, a firstborn son. He'd lived briefly, because of a heart problem, and had died in his parents' arms at only three days old. All who knew the family cried for most of that week. There's an indescribable aching, crushing sort of pain in watching a 20-ft hearse carrying a tiny white coffin. If that's how it felt for those close to the family, I can't begin to imagine what the pain must have been like for the parents.

Some of the hardest things in life are suffering, sickness and pain. In 1650, a Christian minister from Kidderminster called Richard Baxter wrote a book that beautifully describes various aspects of our eternal life: *The Saints' Everlasting Rest*. As in John Owen's work, referred to on pages 19–24, the language is old-fashioned and requires a bit more time to read and understand, but his description is worth the effort. He said, 'A gale of groans and stream of tears accompany us to the very gates [of heaven].'[1] Many of us would acknowledge the truth of that statement from our own personal experience. We cannot hear the news without being acutely aware of the suffering, pain, sickness, poverty, greed, hatred and sadness that blight our world.

The promise of eternal life is not only that we shall experience new levels of beauty and perfection but also that there will be no more sickness, suffering or pain. The Bible speaks of a future day when '"[God] will wipe every tear from their eyes. There will be no more death" or mourning or crying or pain, for the old order of things has passed away' (Revelation 21:4).

The Bible doesn't tell us how such sadness will be removed. It's difficult to imagine that painful memories here will be erased or somehow less painful. This area is one of those in which we take hold of the promise without necessarily understanding the mystery.

Here's what I do know, though. Almost everything you've been told about heaven is wrong. Clouds, harps, pudgy babies with rosy cheeks and blonde curls – all wrong. I've no idea of the origins of these ideas, which seem to appear in anything from old paintings to modern TV adverts for soft cheese. What I am certain of is that none of them appears in the Bible's own description of eternal life.

Yet most of us are unaware of the rich and vivid picture in the Bible, so we think the whole idea of eternal life looks, well, a bit boring. The writer Mark Twain quipped, 'Most people can't bear sitting in church for an hour on a Sunday. How are they supposed to live somewhere very similar to it for an eternity?' In similar vein, the author Isaac Asimov wrote, 'Whatever the tortures of hell, the boredom of heaven would be worse.'[2] Friedrich Nietzsche suggested, 'In heaven all the interesting people are missing.'[3] Is that really what it will be like? Will it be an eternal disembodied boredom?

It's easy to see why people might be uninterested in the afterlife. Yet we can't quite bring ourselves to throw the whole idea out. We still like to think that our loved ones have gone somewhere better. We're just increasingly unsure about where, what and how. I seldom attend a funeral at which there isn't a mention of a deceased loved one who is 'looking down', is in a 'better place' or is still 'with us' in some way.

It all raises the question: if there is eternal life, what is it like?

Eternal life will be physical

There is a lot of confusion, as we've seen, with most of our images coming from popular TV and film portrayals – blue sky, white fluffy clouds, long robes – and, to be honest, it does look pretty underwhelming.

The Bible, however, describes eternal life very differently. Jesus himself speaks about his Father's house – a place with many rooms (which sounds more like a palace than an ordinary house). The last book of the Bible, Revelation, describes a beautiful city with grand walls and gates, and a garden-oasis with a crystal-clear river and fruit-laden trees. Imagine visiting the Palace of Versailles and never having to leave, because it's now become your home.

The apostle and early Christian writer Paul describes how the whole creation awaits its liberation or restoration.[4] This creation, far from being annihilated, it seems, will be restored to even greater heights of beauty and perfection. It will be a return to Eden, home of the first humans, but an Eden that has been cultivated, civilized, restored and made even more beautiful.

One writer describes the relationship of the present creation to the new creation:

> Just as the caterpillar becomes a butterfly, as carbon is converted into diamond, as the grain of wheat upon dying in the ground produces other grains of wheat, as all of nature revives in the spring and dresses up in celebrative clothing . . . so too, by the re-creating power of Christ, the new heaven and the new earth will one day emerge . . . radiant in enduring glory.[5]

I take this to mean that we will still enjoy food, friendship, exercise, the arts, nature and many other things, all to new levels of enjoyment that we can only begin to imagine. It means that I don't need to worry about completing my bucket list in this life. I'll have all eternity to explore and enjoy cultures, cuisines and creation. In *The Great Divorce*, C. S. Lewis vividly describes how the blades of grass initially hurt the feet of new inhabitants of the new creation, precisely because it is somehow *more* physical and our senses are somehow *more* alive to the wonder and beauty of God's creation.[6]

Our eternal life won't be a disembodied floating through space. It will be a physical material existence – we will see, hear, touch, taste and smell – in a place more wonderful than we can ever imagine.

Eternal life will be perfect

Life here is often good but we know it's not perfect. Most of us live with a varying mixture of good and bad, health and ill-health, wealth and want, trial and tribulation. Whatever good we do experience here is not perfection – that still awaits us. The apostle Paul wrote that no eye has seen, no ear has heard, no mind has conceived the things God has prepared for those who love him (1 Corinthians 2:9).

Baxter describes the perfection of God as being like an ocean: 'All good whatsoever is comprised in God and all in the creatures are but drops of this ocean.'[7] Baxter is saying that, in God's new creation, we will experience the perfection of the good things we enjoy on earth. If we think of God's perfection as being like an ocean, our best experiences are a drop in that ocean. Eternal life will be a journey of learning and experiencing more and more of an ocean of perfection.

It may help to think of it another way: I'm short-sighted; without my glasses, I can't see very much. If you were to lead me up a mountain, take my glasses off and tell me to admire the view, I would get a vague sense of the shapes and the colours. But only when I put my glasses back on would I see more of the grandeur and beauty.

If you've ever tried to eat your favourite meal while suffering from a cold, you'll know the frustration and disappointment at not being able to taste it. Perhaps that is an analogy for life now, compared with eternal life. We taste things now in a way that, by comparison, is dull. Then, we shall taste everything just the way it's supposed to be.

It's the difference between ground ginger and fresh, instant coffee and real. You simply can't compare them. The real thing zings and pops in your mouth and your nose. It's the difference between splashing in a paddling pool and swimming in the sea, or between taking your morning shower and standing under a waterfall. One you can do while half-asleep, the other will make you feel truly alive.

We now see only partially all the amazing beauty and perfection that God has in store in the new creation. It is as if we have tasted the hors d'oeuvres, leaving our appetites whetted for the main course.

Eternal life will be . . . eternal

To state the obvious: eternal life will be eternal. But let's consider the implications.

You'll have heard that 'time flies when you're having fun'. I expect that will be true to an infinite degree in the new creation. We sometimes think of eternity as being a really, *really* long time. How then is it that we won't become bored? Our conception of duration and time is rooted in our present existence, in which the passing of time can be subject to frustration and boredom. Eternal life isn't a really, really, *really* long time. It's a different mode of existence.

Currently, we are creatures bound by a particular understanding of time. The Bible tells us that, for the eternal God, a day is like a thousand years and a thousand years like a day.[8] Could it be that, in the new creation, eternity means we won't suffer the frustrations related to the passing of time as we now know it? Whatever our experience, we can be assured that time will never drag. We sometimes encounter those moments that we wish could go on for ever: perhaps hanging out with friends at the beach, enjoying a special meal or a holiday somewhere beautiful. We wish time *would* drag so that we could stay where we are and enjoy it some more. Yet it cannot be. We still have to go home, do the washing-up, iron clothes and get the kids to school the next morning. I suspect our eternal life will be more like that 'moment' of deep joy, peace, happiness and satisfaction, a 'moment' that will last for ever, in which we won't even have to worry about clocks or chores.

The other benefit to *eternal* life is that, unlike the aftermath of a holiday of a lifetime, we'll never have those sad feelings of our joy coming to an end. Here's Richard Baxter again: 'The very thought of once leaving it would else embitter all our joys; and the more would it pierce us because of the singular excellencies which we must forsake.'[9]

In this case, eternity – an eternal future with God – means nothing less than joy without end.

Eternal life will be life with God himself

In April 2020, Father Giuseppe Berardelli died. He'd contracted Covid-19 and had become seriously ill. The people in his church had bought him a ventilator. But he chose to give it to a younger patient, who survived, while he died. Why did Father Berardelli do that? Humans are capable of great sacrifice at times of crisis. I wonder if, in part, it was because he believed that, although death was a fearful thing, it wasn't final.

The best thing about heaven and the new creation is that God himself will be there. That might not excite you as much as the thought of eternity to enjoy beaches, barbecues, mountains and music, but I want to show you that the greatest reward of eternal life is God himself.

Think of it this way. Who do you most enjoy spending time with now? Perhaps it's time alone with a partner, playing with your children, or eating steak and drinking whisky with good mates. What is it about those times together that are so fulfilling and refreshing? I guess it might be the deep conversation, laughing together or just being with someone who understands you and cares about you. There are some people whom we love being around because we can absolutely be ourselves. We don't even have to try. It's just pleasurable and enjoyable. We look forward to such times.

Now, magnify all those feelings by a million; you're still not close to the experience of being with God. He is the one who really gets us, is interested in us, fulfils us and energizes us. We can only begin to imagine what it will be like to have that perfect relationship with God and with one another. It will be totally unspoiled by us or by others. We will know happiness and fulfilment of the kind we've tasted only occasionally and fleetingly. Baxter claims that the highest good of heaven will be knowing more of God's love for us:

> Thou shalt be eternally embraced in the arms of that love, which was from everlasting, and will extend to everlasting; of that love which brought the Son of God's love from heaven to earth, from the earth to the cross, from the cross to the grave, from the grave to glory; that love which was weary, hungry, tempted, scorned, scourged, buffeted, spit upon, crucified, pierced; which did fast, pray, teach, heal, weep, sweat, bleed, die – that love will eternally embrace thee.[10]

Knowing more of the one who made us, sustains, knows and loves us will be the most incredible joy of eternal life. Everything we do will thrill us in as yet unexperienced ways. We will be all that we were meant to be, with no frustration, pain or friction.

Earlier, on page 112, I left out the final part of a quotation from Baxter, and in some ways the most important part. So here it is, this time in full: 'A gale of groans and stream of tears accompany us to the very gates, *and there bid us farewell, for ever.*'[11]

I hope that as you've read this chapter, it's made your heart beat a little faster. Eternal life isn't all harps and halos. It's about being *more* human, perfectly human, in a perfect and beautiful physical world, and enjoying one another, enjoying creation and enjoying God. It will be mind-bendingly beautiful. It will be free from all hurt and harm. Without end.

Here is one final quote from Richard Baxter that is well worth reading and then rereading:

In the meantime, let this much kindle thy desires, and quicken thine endeavours. Up, and be doing; run and strive and fight and hold on, for thou hast a certain, glorious prize before thee. *God will not mock thee: do not mock thyself, nor betray thy soul, by delay or dallying, and all is thine own* . . .[12]

Conclusion:
what next?

For God so loved the world that he gave his one
and only Son, that whoever believes in him shall
not perish but have eternal life.
(John 3:16)

The most famous Bible verse in the world. In every
language, in every nation, on T-shirts, fridge magnets,
calendars, car stickers and coffee cups.

It's a verse that has crossed continents and centuries,
changing millions, if not billions, of lives.

It speaks of love, dignity, destiny, purpose and hope.
It's light in the darkness, food for the hungry, water for
the thirsty, comfort for the hurting and strength for the
weary.

It's the most significant claim in the entire history of
the human race.

I hope that my explanation has illustrated why it's so
important and so cherished. And I hope that you can
see how these twenty-six words can change your life and
your whole world.

A friend of mine was gazing out of his study window.
He spotted a blackbird hopping along a slender branch

before flying off to another tree. Moments later, a large pigeon attempted to land on the same slender branch. As it landed, the entire branch began to bend under its weight, forcing it to fly off and find somewhere sturdier to rest.

Some things in this world aren't made to bear the weight of our deepest needs, hopes, desires and dreams. Career success, financial wealth and relationships can't support the burden that is composed of our deepest longings. They will simply bend and break under the weight of expectation.

By contrast, God's promise can bear our weight. God's love can meet our deepest desire for belonging and acceptance. God's Son can meet our deepest need for forgiveness and peace. God's future can meet our deepest hope for happiness and security. It simply requires us to stop flapping around and place our feet on the solid ground of this promise.

When the boy cried 'wolf' for the third time, no-one came running. They'd heard it before. They thought they knew what was happening, so they ignored the call. Perhaps you've heard this message before. Maybe you'll put down this book and quietly move on. Perhaps, this time, you'll give Jesus a second look.

The Christian faith really is worth considering and investigating – so many have discovered that. Who cares what others might say or think? It is too important for pride to get in the way.

I urge you to discover the greatest treasure this world affords.

For God so loved the world that he gave his one and only Son, that whoever believes in him shall not perish but have eternal life.

Prayer

Although the idea of prayer may seem strange if you've never done it before, God invites us to speak to him, promising that he hears us.

Here's a model that you can use when you pray:

Our Father, thank you for your love for me. Thank you for sending Jesus to die for my sin. Thank you for the promise of eternal life.

Father, I believe it. I believe it all. I believe that Jesus is Lord, that he died for me and that he is risen from the dead.

Father, I know that I've shunned you and your love in many ways. I turn from that now and ask you to forgive me for my sins.

Father, I receive you as my King, Saviour and friend. Help me now to live my life for you.
Amen.

Notes

1 For God . . .

1 The full interview can be found at 'God, the universe and meaning' [video], YouTube (recorded and uploaded 13 January 2018), <www.youtube.com/watch?v=6iVbBd9h7W8>, accessed 15 March 2021.

2 This is an argument made by a philosopher called William Paley. See Peter S. Williams, *A Faithful Guide to Philosophy: A Christian introduction to the love of wisdom* (Milton Keynes: Paternoster, 2013), p. 110.

3 Anthony Flew, *There Is a God: How the world's most notorious atheist changed his mind* (New York, NY: HarperOne, 2007), p. 96.

4 These illustrations are used by Fred Hoyle in *The Intelligent Universe* (New York, NY: Holt, Rinehart & Winston, 1983).

5 Cited in Flew, *There Is a God*, p. 99.

6 C. S. Lewis, *Mere Christianity* (London: HarperCollins, 2002), p. 6.

7 Friedrich Nietzsche, *On the Genealogy of Morals* (New York, NY: Dover, 2003), p. 25.

8 Nietzsche, *On the Genealogy of Morals*, p. 25.

9 G. K. Chesterton, *The Everlasting Man* (San Francisco, CA: Ignatius Press, 1993), pp. 27–34.

10 Benjamin Zander, 'The transformative power
    of classical music' [video], TED Talks (2008),
    <www.ted.com/talks/benjamin_zander_on_music_
    and_passion>, accessed 15 March 2021.

2 So loved . . .

 1 The full list can be found in Traci Lester,
    '30 Hilarious insights from kids about love and
    marriage' [blog], goodreads (13 February 2016),
    <www.goodreads.com/author_blog_posts/9917475-
    30-hilarious-insights-from-kids-about-love-and-
    marriage>, accessed 15 March 2021.
 2 Office for National Statistics, 'Divorce' (n.d.),
    <www.ons.gov.uk/peoplepopulationandcommunity/
    birthsdeathsandmarriages/divorce>, accessed
    15 March 2021.
 3 Rachel Schraer, 'The blame game: getting divorced in
    the UK', BBC News (27 May 2018), <www.bbc.co.uk/
    news/uk-44253225>, accessed 15 March 2021.
 4 Garry J. Williams, *His Love Endures For Ever: Reflections
    on the love of God* (Nottingham: IVP, 2015), p. 10.
 5 John Owen, 'The death of death', in *The Death of
    Christ*, vol. 10 of *The Works of John Owen* (Edinburgh:
    Banner of Truth, 1967; repr. 2000), p. 323.
 6 Sam McBratney, *Guess How Much I Love You*
    (Somerville, MA: Candlewick Press, 2013).
 7 Williams, *His Love Endures for Ever*, p. 133.
 8 C. S. Lewis, *God in the Dock* (Grand Rapids, MI:
    Eerdmans, 1970), p. 49.
 9 John Owen, 'The death of death', p. 323.

3 The world . . .

1 See Luke 18:9–14.
2 Kate Fox, *Watching the English: The hidden rules of English behaviour* (London: Hodder & Stoughton, 2004), pp. 400–415.
3 To paraphrase the poem 'Invictus' by William Ernest Henley.
4 Francis Spufford, *Unapologetic: Why, despite everything, Christianity can still make surprising emotional sense* (London: Faber & Faber, 2012), pp. 27–28.
5 Augustine, *Confessions*, tr. Albert Outler (New York, NY: Dover, 2002), p. 26.
6 See Matthew 7:3–4.
7 Cornelius Plantinga Jr, 'Sin: not the way it's supposed to be' [online PDF], p. 11, <http://tgc-documents.s3.amazonaws.com/cci/Pantinga.pdf>, accessed 15 March 2021.
8 Cited in Cornelius Plantinga Jr, *Engaging God's World: A Christian vision of faith, learning, and living* (Grand Rapids, MI: Eerdmans, 2002), p. 54.
9 Plantinga, *Engaging God's World*, p. 57.

4 That he gave . . .

1 James S. Jeffers, *The Greco-Roman World of the New Testament Era: Exploring the background of early Christianity* (Downers Grove, IL: IVP, 1999), pp. 192–193.
2 Jeffers, *The Greco-Roman World*, pp. 192–193.

3 *Corpus Inscriptionum Latinarum*, 4.9839b, cited in Jeffers, *The Greco-Roman World,* p. 193.

4 The core beliefs and practices of Islam: the declaration of faith (*shahada*), prayer (*salah*), alms-giving (*zakat*), fasting (*sawm*) and pilgrimage (*hajj*).

5 This owes more to Dante's *Purgatorio* than to anything written in the Bible.

6 The eightfold path consists of right understanding, right thought, right speech, right action, right livelihood (that is, earning a living without harming anything living), right effort, right mindfulness and right concentration.

7 Jonathan Aitken, *John Newton: From disgrace to amazing grace* (London: Continuum, 2007), p. xiii.

8 John Newton, 'An authentic narrative', in *The Works of the Rev. John Newton* (Edinburgh: Ross & Co., 1839), p. 11.

9 Aitken, *John Newton*, pp. xiii–xiv.

10 Aitken, *John Newton*, pp. 161–167.

5 His one and only Son . . .

1 C. S. Lewis, *Mere Christianity* (London: HarperCollins, 2002), p. 52.

2 John Stott, *The Cross of Christ*, 2nd edn (Leicester: IVP, 1989; repr. 2003), p. 160.

3 If you want to read more about this, see Lee Strobel, *The Case for Easter: A journalist investigates the evidence for the resurrection* (Grand Rapids, MI: Zondervan, 2009).

4 Malcolm Muggeridge, *Jesus: The Man Who Lives*
  (New York, NY: Harper & Row, 1975), pp. 98–100.
5 I'm indebted for this illustration to a lecture given by
  Chris Stead, 'Humanity in theology', Oak Hill School
  of Theology, July 2019.

6 That whoever . . .

1 Matt Bonesteel, 'President Trump says Stephen
  Curry's White House invitation has been
  "withdrawn"', *Washington Post* (23 September 2017),
  <www.washingtonpost.com/news/early-lead/
  wp/2017/09/23/president-trump-says-stephen-currys-
  white-house-invitation-has-been-withdrawn/
  ?utm_term=.839599f731c7>, accessed 15 March
  2021.
2 See Luke 23:26–43.
3 Tim Townsend, 'Opinion: the amazing story of U.S.
  Army chaplains who ministered to Nazi leaders at
  Nuremberg trials 70 years ago today', *Washington Post*
  (20 November 2015), <www.washingtonpost.com/
  news/acts-of-faith/wp/2015/11/20/the-amazing-
  story-of-u-s-army-chaplains-who-ministered-to-
  nazi-leaders-at-the-nuremberg-trials-70-years-ago-
  today/?utm_term=.236af77f814f>, accessed 15 March
  2021.
4 'Henry F. Gerecke', Wikipedia (last modified 3 March
  2021), <https://en.wikipedia.org/wiki/Henry_F._
  Gerecke>, accessed 15 March 2021.
5 Cited in Denis Campbell, 'One in five young women
  have self-harmed, study reveals', *The Guardian*

(4 June 2019), <www.theguardian.com/society/2019/
jun/04/one-in-five-young-women-have-self-harmed-
study-reveals>, accessed 15 March 2021.

6 Campbell, 'One in five young women'.

7 Roald Dahl, *Charlie and the Chocolate Factory*
(London: Puffin Books, 2007), p. 143.

8 Abbey Stone, '11 greatest pranks of all time', Mental
Floss (1 April 2017), <http://mentalfloss.com/
article/62676/11-greatest-pranks-all-time>, accessed
15 March 2021.

9 If you want to read more about the historical evidence
for Christianity, you could start with Lee Strobel, *The
Case for Christ: A journalist's personal investigation of
the evidence for Jesus* (Grand Rapids, MI: Zondervan,
2016) or Peter J. Williams, *Can We Trust the Gospels?*
(Wheaton, IL: Crossway, 2018).

7 Believes . . .

1 *Miracle on 34th Street* (1994), Director: Les Mayfield.

2 Bertrand Russell, *Human Society in Ethics and
Politics* (London: Allen & Unwin, 1954), p. 215.

3 Sam Harris, *Letter to a Christian Nation: A challenge
to the faith of America* (London: Bantam, 2007), p. 67.

4 A. C. Grayling. *Against All Gods: Six polemics on
religion and an essay on kindness* (London: Oberon,
2007), pp. 15–16.

5 J. P. Moreland, *Kingdom Triangle: Recover the
Christian mind, renovate the soul, restore the Spirit's
power* (Grand Rapids, MI: Zondervan, 2007), p. 124;
cited in Peter S. Williams, *A Faithful Guide*

to Philosophy: A Christian introduction to the love of wisdom (Milton Keynes: Paternoster, 2013), p. 15.

6 J. P. Moreland, 'Living smart', in Paul Copan and William Lane Craig (eds.) *Passionate Conviction: Contemporary discourses on Christian apologetics* (Nashville, TN: B&H Academic, 2007), 22; cited in Williams, *A Faithful Guide*, p. 15.

7 See John 20:30–31.

8 See 1 Corinthians 15:6.

9 See Acts 26:26.

10 C. S. Lewis, *Mere Christianity* (London: HarperCollins, 2002), pp. 138–150.

11 Lewis, *Mere Christianity*, pp. 140–141.

12 G. K. Chesterton, 'The book of Job', in Alberto Manguel (ed.), *On Lying in Bed and Other Essays by G. K. Chesterton* (Calgary: Bayeux Arts, 2000), p. 176.

13 C. S. Lewis, *Mere Christianity*, pp. 142–143.

8 In him . . .

1 *Daylight* (1996) is a film in which a tunnel underneath New York's Hudson River collapses, letting in water. It takes a nail-biting couple of hours to see if the main characters will escape before it's too late. Director: Rob Cohen.

2 Lesslie Newbigin, *The Gospel in a Pluralist Society* (London: SPCK, 1989), p. 170.

3 If you would like to examine the evidence for the reliability of the Gospel accounts more closely, see Peter J. Williams, *Can We Trust the Gospels?* (Wheaton, IL: Crossway, 2018).

4 Some of the material in the following paragraphs is inspired by a talk given by Tim Keller entitled 'Exclusivity: how can there be just one true religion?' [audio], YouTube (recorded 24 September 2006, uploaded 10 August 2015), <https://www.youtube.com/watch?v=75qetP4dRAA>, accessed 15 March 2021.

9 Shall not perish . . .

1 Reni Eddo-Lodge, *Why I'm No Longer Talking to White People about Race* (London: Bloomsbury, 2018), p. 221.

2 Tom Wright, *Surprised by Hope* (London: SPCK, 2007), p. 192.

3 Wright, *Surprised by Hope*, p. 192.

4 Aldous Huxley, *Brave New World* (London: Harper Perennial, 2006).

5 *The Good Place* (2016–2020), NBC, Executive Producers: Michael Schur, David Miner, Morgan Sackett, Drew Goddard.

6 Aleksandr Solzhenitsyn, *The Gulag Archipelago* (London: Collins, 1974), p. 168.

7 *Police Interceptors*, Channel 5 (2008 to present).

8 This is a paraphrase; see John 8:7.

9 This is a paraphrase; see Matthew 7:5 and Luke 6:42.

10 See, for example, the vision that Isaiah has of God in the temple: Isaiah 6:1–5.

10 But have eternal life

1 Richard Baxter, *The Saints' Everlasting Rest* (Vancouver: Regent College, 1962), p. 39.

2 Both cited in Randy Alcorn, *50 Days of Heaven: Reflections that bring eternity to light* (Carol Stream, IL.: Tyndale House Publishers, 2006), p. 237.

3 Cited in Chester Dolan, *Religion on Trial: With 800 material witnesses* (Lakewood, CA: Mopah, 2002), p. 91.

4 You can read more in John 14, Revelation 21 – 22 and Romans 8.

5 Herman Bavinck, *Reformed Dogmatics, Volume 4: Holy Spirit, Church, and New Creation* (Grand Rapids, MI: Baker Academic, 2008), p. 720.

6 C. S. Lewis, *The Great Divorce* (London: HarperCollins, 2015), p. 25.

7 Baxter, *The Saints' Everlasting Rest*, p. 40.

8 See 2 Peter 3.8.

9 Baxter, *The Saints' Everlasting Rest*, p. 82.

10 Baxter, *The Saints' Everlasting Rest*, p. 45.

11 Baxter, *The Saints' Everlasting Rest*, p. 39; emphasis mine.

12 Baxter, *The Saints' Everlasting Rest*, p. 83; emphasis mine.